20

A

LORCA: THE DRAWINGS

LORCA

THE DRAWINGS

THEIR RELATION TO THE POET'S LIFE AND WORK

HELEN OPPENHEIMER, 1945-

FRANKLIN WATTS
NEW YORK TORONTO
1987

First published in Great Britain in 1986
by The Herbert Press Limited

First published in the United States in 1987
by Franklin Watts, Inc., 387 Park Avenue South,
New York, New York 10016.

ISBN 0–531–15034–8

Printed and bound in Great Britain

CONTENTS

ACKNOWLEDGEMENTS

The main theme of this book was originally the subject of my Ph.D thesis. I am therefore much indebted to the considerable help and guidance which I received from Professor J. E. Varey of Westfield College, London. In the 1960s I met Lorca's brother Francisco García Lorca and his wife Laura de los Ríos, both now sadly deceased; they put at my disposal a considerable amount of material. Lorca's sister, Isabel García Lorca, has also provided me with tireless support in this project, as has her nephew Manuel Fernández-Montesinos and his sister Tica Fernández-Montesinos. To them all I offer my sincere thanks.

Much more than moral support has come from Ian Gibson, whose brilliant and exhaustive biography of Lorca is unsurpassable and will soon be published in English. Ian Gibson has shown extraordinary generosity in sharing material which he alone uncovered over many years of diligent study. I doubt whether this book would have developed at all without the stimulus and kindness of this most gifted scholar.

Many other hispanists and *lorquistas* have helped me on my way; it would be impossible to name them all. Marie Laffranque, Mario Hernández, Andrew Anderson, Brian Morris, Eutimio Martín, Rafael Martínez Nadal, Gregorio Prieto, Antonio Gallego-Morell, have all taken time to think about this project and have given me much help and advice, for which I am more than grateful.

I should also like to thank the Lorca family for loaning me drawings for reproduction from their private collection, and for other copyright material. Gregorio Prieto, Rafael Martínez Nadal and Eutimio Martín have all been most generous in contributing material for the illustrations. Other drawings have been reproduced with the permission of the Lorca Estate and the help of the Fundación García Lorca. I am grateful to John Lawrence-Jones for photographing many of the drawings.

Finally I should like to thank my children, Sarah and Russell, for putting up with my frequent trips to Spain; my husband Ralph whose constant

ACKNOWLEDGEMENTS

support and encouragement has made this book possible; my publisher David Herbert and his wife Brenda whose endless patience and meticulous attention to detail have helped me to achieve something I have always wanted to do.

Numbers in brackets in the text refer to the illustrations; c indicates colour plates. The reference numbers after the quotations from Lorca's written work refer to the *Obras completas*. All the translations are mine; they are deliberately more literal than poetic; I strongly recommend reading the original Spanish whenever possible.

Helen Oppenheimer 1986

INTRODUCTION

Federico García Lorca is probably better known internationally than any other Spanish poet, though his reputation has changed with ensuing generations. In the period immediately after the Spanish Civil War and his tragic murder by the fascists, he had already become something of a legend both in Spain and abroad and was regarded by many as a political martyr. In Britain and America, especially, he was widely read, both in his own tongue and in translation. More recently, his plays *Yerma* and *Bodas de sangre* (Blood Wedding) have been increasingly performed, and *Bodas de sangre* has been transformed into a ballet. His reputation as a poet, too, has grown and changed with the advent and appreciation of a new generation to whom the Spanish Civil War is part of history. Nowadays, Lorca is no longer regarded merely as a gifted cult figure, but is firmly established as one of the great writers of the twentieth century.

Lorca's talents, however, were not only literary. Like all great men, he was capable of expressing himself in many different ways. He was an accomplished pianist and composer and his musicianship has been widely recognized. What is not generally known is that he was a prolific and ambitious visual artist who left behind him a large number of fascinating drawings and sketches. His graphic work is the most neglected aspect of this modern 'Renaissance' man.

Lorca drew constantly throughout his life, both formally and informally. Some drawings were sketched rapidly on pieces of writing paper, to capture a moment, and then given to friends. His legendary generosity makes it difficult to trace much of his work, and often nothing is known of a drawing or a design until the owner discloses its existence. Sometimes Lorca decorated his letters with drawings to liven up his correspondence. Some of his drawings are ambitious, betraying hours of patient planning and dedication. It is estimated that there must be about four hundred drawings still in existence.

Most of them are executed in pen and ink or coloured pencils. They are usually fairly small in size, not exceeding an average manuscript page. The variety of subject and style is remarkable, but they can be classified roughly into three groups.

Early in his life, Lorca was recording the world around him in visual experiments and sketches: vases of flowers, bowls of fruit, balcony scenes and patios. In this category we can also place his many cubist drawings, which reveal his interest in contemporary art movements.

The literary drawings relate closely to the poems and have much greater symbolic value. They are the most interesting to analyse. Often a drawing can help to decipher an image in a poem that would otherwise remain obscure. In this group I also include drawings related to recurring leit-motifs in all his work: the themes of communication, sex, death and religion, which obsessed the artist throughout his life.

The third group consists of the theatre drawings which relate to Lorca's lifelong passion for the stage. They show that he not only created the dialogue for his plays but also envisaged the entire production, including the appearance of the actors. These drawings are very detailed, colourful, and aesthetically pleasing.

This book is an attempt to introduce a wider public to his drawings and to relate them to Lorca's life and the great body of his written work. Where a drawing cannot be dated, it is treated thematically, linking it to a particular period of his development.

Lorca's biographers have variously compared his graphic work to Ingres' violin, or to a 'secret love' which he kept by his side. The truth is that for Lorca drawing was more than just a hobby or whimsical pastime. Because he was not trained as a draughtsman he had a very direct and unsophisticated way of expressing himself in line and colour. The visual images he created often contain the germ of an idea which he later elaborated in a sophisticated piece of writing. They are not mere decoration. They are a key to understanding the man and his literary achievements.

These drawings are simultaneously pure poetry and pure art.
I feel myself to be clean, comforted, happy,
childlike, when I do them. I am horrified by the
painting they call direct, which is no more
than an anguished battle with form in which the painter
always emerges vanquished and with the work dead . . .
Moreover, I would call these drawings . . . very human
drawings. Because nearly all of them strike a
little arrow in the heart.

Federico García Lorca (OC 1659)

ANDALUSIAN DRAWINGS

**Federico study! All he did
was draw, filling his notebooks with
figures and caricatures.**

Joaquín Alemán (Headmaster)

Federico García Lorca was born on 5 June 1898 in the village of Fuente Vaqueros, some 18 km from Granada, in one of the world's most beautiful agricultural regions. The *vega* or open plain of Granada is situated about 50 km from the sea, separated from it by the Sierra Nevada, and enjoys abundant sunshine as well as water from the river Genil. It is not surprising that when the Moors came over to the south of Spain in 711 they thought they were in Paradise.

Federico's family on his father's side had lived in this part of Spain for several generations. His relations were for the most part lively and exceptional people, talented musicians and keen readers of literature.

Federico's father was already thirty-seven and a widower when he married Vicenta Lorca Romero, a primary schoolteacher from Granada. The marriage was much frowned upon by don Federico's brothers, because he was already a wealthy farmer and doña Vicenta had nothing but her personality and talents. She was to become a dominant figure in her family's life. Lorca said that he remembered her organizing the whole household, waking the children very early every morning with a little prayer. At this time his father would have already gone off to the fields, where he would remain until nightfall. Doña Vicenta must also have nurtured the young Federico's passion for music, for although she did not play any musical instrument, she was an avid collector of classical records, which naturally her children listened to as well. In later years Federico claimed that he had inherited his passion and his spirit from his father but that his intelligence and sensibility came from his mother. He was to use his mother's surname – Lorca – more than his father's, as García was a very common name.

The children numbered five altogether but Lorca's younger brother Luis died at the age of two, when Federico was four years old. Francisco (Paco) was born in 1902, followed by María de la Concepción (Concha) in 1903 and then, after a long gap, Isabel in 1910. Being the eldest son of a large family, with more than forty cousins, Federico enjoyed the security and attention that this position gave him. In 1928 he wrote: 'My childhood consisted of learning literature and music with my mother, being a little rich boy in the village, a bossyboots.'

The inhabitants of Fuente Vaqueros were cheerful, open people, liberal minded and somewhat anti-clerical. As a child Federico had a physical disability in his legs that made him unable to run easily with other children. This did not affect his popularity, for he was a highly imaginative child, often conducting complicated fantasy games with the local children. But his inability to run may have accelerated his mental development. From a very early age Federico felt closely identified with nature. He would engage in conversation with the insects and plants, and he recalled one occasion when he thought the trees were calling out his name, 'Fe...de...ri...co...', but it was only the rustling of the poplar leaves in the wind.

One of Federico's favourite childhood games was to improvise Mass in the back garden. He would place a picture of the Virgin and some roses from the garden on an old wall in the patio, and then summon his brother and sisters and his mother to be the congregation while he, draped in flowing robes, would recite the Mass with great conviction. He would insist on his mother crying during the sermon and she never failed to do so. Federico's appreciation of the mass as 'theatre' is borne out by the fact that as soon as he had seen his first puppet show, he adapted the 'altar' in his garden into a little stage.

His childhood vision of religion reappears in his adult work. The highly decorated drawing of the Virgin of the Seven Swords (C10) celebrates local festivity rather than a profound religious experience. The naive way in which he has drawn the olive trees and crosses on the hillside underlines his delight in the popular aspect of religion, the street-fair atmosphere of the religious processions. There was a procession every year in Fuente Vaqueros in early September when the Victory Christ, the patron of the village, was carried through the streets accompanied by fireworks.

1 Set for *Mariana Pineda*

Federico loved this occasion as a child, and as a grown man always tried to return to Fuente Vaqueros for it.

Other drawings of figures (8, c6, c7, c8) also show his enjoyment of beauty and theatricality. It is interesting that many of the figures are dressed in a similar way: a short tunic with decorated pantaloons underneath, as worn by the female dancer (c3), the little girls (1) and the young bard (c8). Could there be a bisexual allusion in this costume? Certainly this is no ordinary dress; these are garments worn for a special occasion, and all those who wear it are entertainers. (Lorca may have seen costume designs for the Diaghilev Ballet, some of which also bear a marked resemblance to this type of dress.)

2 Motherhood

In spite of affluent circumstances, Federico was also very aware of the poverty that existed in his village. He would play with children from all walks of life. One of his playmates was a little girl whose father was a piece-work labourer; when he had no work his children had to share clothes, so that some of them went naked, and all of them starved. Federico's radical views in later life, in sympathy with the underprivileged, were nurtured from these early experiences. At the age of seven he had his first intimate experience of death. A shepherd who had been a great friend of his died at the age of fifty-five. The whole family attended the funeral procession to the cemetery. This solemn event made a great impression on the young boy, who actually saw the corpse. In years to come he would describe in vivid detail the decomposition and putrefaction of corpses.

The representation of putrefaction is another common theme of Lorca's drawings, especially later in his life (61, 62, C27). Often figures are drawn in the act of vomiting and with a similar decomposition coming from the genital area. A worm-like substance representing death is often drawn on its own, or the worms are personified to represent people and plants (48, 51).

In 1907, when Lorca was nine, the whole family moved to Asquerosa (later called Valderrubio) and his idyllic rural childhood in Fuente Vaqueros came to an end. But the seeds had been sown. Lorca was imbued with a taste for the earth, the seasons of the year, the insects, the animals, the peasants. 'I have an agrarian complex' he said, years later. He claimed that he would never have been able to write his play *Bodas de sangre* had it not been for his early years in Fuente Vaqueros.

At the age of ten, he was due to start studying for his *bachillerato* (final school exams) and his parents sent him to board at the house of his first schoolmaster Antonio Rodríguez Espinosa, with whom they had kept in touch, in Almería. Don Antonio was a progressive teacher who believed that education should be practical and relevant to everyday life. He had been much influenced by the ideas of the Institución Libre de Enseñanza, the most progressive educational institution in Spain. Some of Federico's cousins were also at don Antonio's house so he was not on his own. It is uncertain how long he stayed there, probably one or two years. Apparently he suffered a severe mouth and throat infection, which caused his face to swell up dramatically, so his parents took him home.

In the summer of 1909 the whole family moved from Asquerosa to Granada, where there were local schools. Federico's brother Francisco commented that there was no violent break with their rural childhood when they moved to Granada because they were often visited by relatives and friends from Fuente Vaqueros, and one of their servants, Dolores Cuesta, joined them in Granada. She was a great 'character', quite illiterate but full of life. Lorca modelled many of his theatrical creations on her, including the maid in *Doña Rosita*, a person of more wordly experience and common sense than her mistress. He had great respect for such servants who, he claimed, were the salt of the earth and gave a sense of identity to spoilt little rich boys like himself. In 1928 Lorca gave a lecture on *Las nanas infantiles* (Children's Nursery Rhymes) expressing his gratitude to people like Dolores who hand down an oral tradition from generation to generation.

The drawing of mother and child (2) relates to his interest in nursery songs and the importance of childhood. He believed that true communication only exists between mother and child, and that thereafter people become more and more isolated. Lorca loved his warm and enveloping childhood, a theme which he constantly recalls in his early poems.

Granada at that time was a small provincial town of 75,000 inhabitants. It had been the prosperous capital city of the Moslem Empire in Spain but had gone into decline after the Moors had been expelled in 1492, taking their agricultural expertise with them. But by 1900 Granada was experiencing an economic revival with the advent of the sugar revolution, mainly the planting of beet. There was considerable reconstruction in the city, some of it for the worse.

From his time in Granada Lorca acquired a love of small and intricate detail which is very much a feature of Arab art. This love of detail is expressed as a poetic concept in his talk *Imaginación, inspiración, evasión*, given in 1928:

> People's imaginations have invented giants to whom they impute the construction of great grottoes or enchanted cities. Reality has shown that these huge grottoes were built by a drop of water. By that drop of pure water, patient and eternal. In this case, as in others, reality wins.

> (OC 87)

Lorca demonstrates that reality is poetic, in other words that the source of poetry is reality and, more precisely, the small things in reality. This appreciation of detail can be seen in the way he decorates his drawings, using ornament for its own sake, as pure poetry (8, C2, C3, C6, C7, C8, C9). In 1936 Lorca spoke openly in favour of the Moslems, in spite of what was taught in the schools. He lamented the loss of their architecture, their knowledge of astronomy, their poetry. The Moslem Empire, he claimed, gave way to a poor and cowardly people, the worst bourgeoisie in Spain. Such harsh words did not earn him the love of many *granadinos*; some people think that they were partly responsible for his death.

Andalusia also introduced Lorca to the gypsy people, with whom he maintained a life-long sympathy. In 1499 the gypsies in Spain had been ordered to give up their nomadic life, and many of them settled in the caves of Sacro Monte on the outskirts of Granada, where they still live. They were threatened with all sorts of penalties, including expulsion, the aim of which was to force them to lose their identity, a theme which Lorca emphasized in *Romancero gitano* (Gypsy Ballads):

> But I am no longer myself
> nor is my house my own.
>
> (OC 431)

In Granada Lorca went to a private school, the Colegio del Sagrado Corazón de Jesús. This was not a religious school, as its name might suggest, but was chosen because it was run by his mother's cousin, Joaquín Alemán. By all accounts Federico was not a good student. Contemporaries of his have recounted how he did little work, mainly because he was just not interested. Joaquín Alemán himself often said that the young Lorca spent all his time drawing, filling his notebooks with figures and caricatures. Alemán also describes him as having a sweet nature, easy-going, almost girlish. This gentleness provoked some teasing from his companions who nicknamed him 'Federica'; and some aggressively masculine teachers rejected him altogether. All this helped to develop a certain independence of mind in the young Lorca; he saw himself as different from the crowd.

Federico's real passion at this time was for music. There are drawings of musical instruments (41, 42), quickly executed but nevertheless revealing a love of the subject. (It is significant that he considered pursuing a musical career in Paris before he thought of himself as a poet.) His teacher was don Antonio Segura Mesa, an aspiring opera composer and a disciple of Verdi. The musical taste of Granada at that time was very sophisticated, and don Antonio started a conservatory with the singer Ronconi. He was clearly no ordinary piano teacher, and Lorca was strongly influenced by his taste and vision. He also cultivated Lorca's interest in folkloric art, which had been awakened by the people of Fuente Vaqueros.

Lorca's drawings record a variety of Andalusian types: an intense-looking gypsy woman (3), women wearing mantillas (5, C5), a girl waiting in a patio (9), a brigand (10), and a young man (11). The language of the Andalusian people is also often recorded in the drawings, more than in the poetry. In many parts of rural Spain people often substitute the letter 'l' for 'r'. Hence Lorca writes *cualto* instead of *cuarto* (C2) and *alte* instead of *arte*, *mielda* instead of *mierda*, *celveza* instead of *cerveza* (C3).

The Spanish educational system at that time allowed a student in his final year of secondary studies for the *bachillerato* to attend the first-year classes of the university, and this Lorca did. His choice of courses was limited, since it was clear that he would not want to study science or medicine, so he took arts and law, which had a common foundation course.

The main influence on Lorca while he was at university was that of don Martín Dominguez Berrueta, a rather innovatory lecturer on the theory of literature and art, who believed that a lecturer should strike up an informal and friendly relationship with his students so that they should benefit from his knowledge and understanding. This attitude differed radically from that of most lecturers who maintained a formal distance from their pupils. Don Martín used to organize study trips, travelling with a number of students around Spain to look at monuments and works of art.

In term-time Berrueta would take his students to visit buildings of architectural interest in Granada. He loved convents, and a visit to Santa Isabel la Real made a particular impression on all the students. The convent was extremely pretty with a tall elegant tower, but what really captured

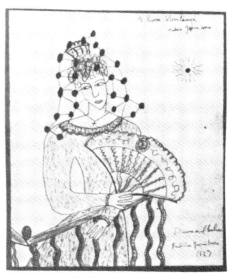

4 *Dama en el balcón* (Lady on the balcony)

3 The madwoman of the circus

5 *Mujer de los madroños* (Woman with spotted mantilla – dedicated to Ana María Dalí)

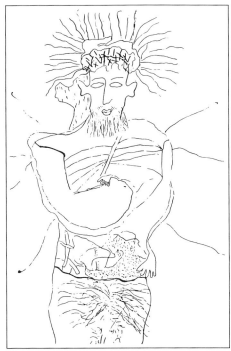

6 Fallen angel

7 St Joseph

the students' imagination was a small dank patio with a little fountain at one side. Lorca made many drawings of patios with fountains, perhaps remembering this one.

The convent is a recurring theme both in his drawings and in his poetry and plays, as, for example, in *La monja gitana* (The Gypsy Nun) and the ending of *Mariana Pineda* (13) where the heroine is incarcerated in a convent before her execution. The nun alone in a garden next to a tomb-stone (12) seems to express Lorca's regret for those who give up their souls and bodies for an abstraction. Lorca believed that the only Christian concept worth adhering to was charity. Perhaps ironically, he had little time for sacrifice and martyrdom.

On his second trip with Berrueta, Lorca visited more convents. What chiefly made an impression on him was the motive that prompted these women to shut themselves off from society and, more, from marriage and

8 St George

9 Young girl

10 Brigand

11 Young man

motherhood. He could understand the appeal of the cloistered life as a refuge for women who did not have the strength to cope with the world, and saw the convent as a huge cold heart wherein these women escape from life and what are considered mortal sins.

There was at this time an arts club called The Artistic and Literary Centre of Granada. Controversy raged between the conservative element, who were closely identified with traditional sentimental poetry that wallowed in Granada's oriental past, and the young writers who despised the Centre for having become bourgeois. Although Lorca was profoundly influenced by the legacy of the Arab world around him, he knew the dangers of being sucked into the orientalist tradition. There are many allusions to gardens and running water in his work, but he rarely mentions the Alhambra. Nevertheless he joined this club, fully understanding the rift that existed there.

He used to play the piano at the Artistic Centre, and it was through his musical talent that he met Fernando de los Ríos, professor of politics at the university, a very civilized man who had studied at the Institución Libre de Enseñanza. Don Fernando, who was to become an important influence on Lorca, heard him playing a Beethoven sonata with great sensitivity; he introduced himself and they became firm friends. In 1937, after Lorca's assassination, when don Fernando was Ambassador of the Spanish Republic to the United States, he made a speech to commemorate the poet's death in which he described himself as the poet's second father.

The young *literati* of Granada channelled their energies into bringing out a literary magazine called *Andalucía 1915* in which they expressed their views on art and published extracts from their own works. They would meet every evening at the Cafe Alameda, in the centre of town. The cafe was populated in the day-time by the bullfighting and market crowd, but at night it became very 'cultured'. A chamber orchestra played classical music, and behind the rostrum there was a large corner section with two or three tables and chairs, and some sofas against a wall, where this group of intellectuals assembled. They named it El Rinconcillo (the little corner). The group flourished between 1915 and 1922. It gathered together the most talented young men of Granada, about seventeen members in all, with some additional 'honorary' and 'visiting' members.

The most prominent personality of the Rinconcillo was Francisco

12 Nun in a garden   13 *Mariana Pineda*

Soriano Lapesa, a vast man with a pale face (the result of an inherited metabolic disorder) and dank, dark hair, who affected an air of decadence similar to Oscar Wilde's. He was a brilliant scholar with two degrees and a doctorate, and eventually obtained the Chair of Arab Studies in Granada. His enormous library contained many erotic and pornographic books. Lorca became quite friendly with this extrovert and exotic character, although Lapesa was one of the first people to observe that Lorca might be *invertido* (homosexual) and this upset Lorca greatly.

Another friend, Ramón Pérez Rodá, was very highly strung and a brilliant mathematician. It was in his house that the Rinconcillistas produced the first exhibition of Lorca's drawings in 1922 or 1923. Apparently this first exhibition was followed by another, but both were fairly local affairs for friends, of which there are no public records.

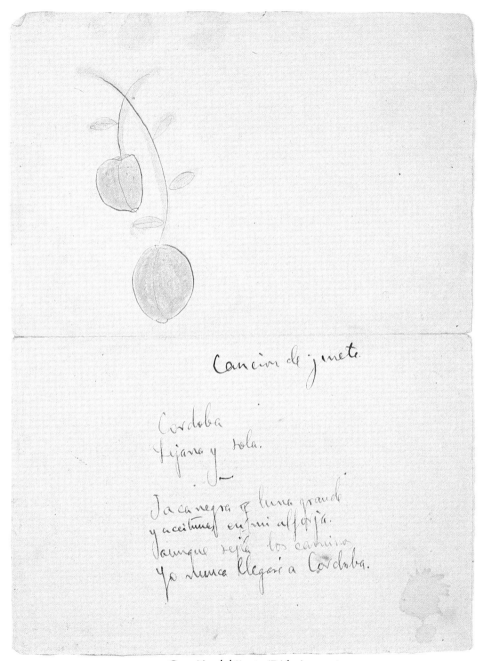

Canción de jinete.

Córdoba
Lejana y sola.

Jaca negra, luna grande,
y aceitunas en mi alforja.
Aunque sepa los caminos
yo nunca llegaré a Córdoba.

CI *Canción del jinete* (Rider's song)

One of the more amusing things that the Rinconcillistas did was to invent a fictitious poet called Isidoro Capdepón Fernández. He wrote in an appallingly sentimental style, but his works were nevertheless eventually published and commented on by critics, much to the delight of the Rinconcillistas. They pushed their joke a little too far when one of Isidoro's poems was dedicated to a known living author, Juan Antonio Cavestany. The poem referred to the good times they had spent together in Uruguay, and Cavestany replied in no uncertain terms that he had never heard of Isidoro Capdepón!

Lorca's clever friends at the Rinconcillo were to create an irreparable rift between himself and his beloved friend and teacher from Granada University, don Martín Domínguez Berrueta. Don Martín had awakened in Lorca a genuine appreciation of art. Lorca had made a trip with him to Burgos and had stayed on there alone with him for a month, and much of what Lorca put into his first published work *Impresiones y paisajes* (Impressions and Landscapes, 1918), was a result of this trip. But when he read extracts to his friends at the Rinconcillo, they said it sounded derivative, pure Berrueta. Lorca allowed himself to be influenced and ended up printing negative criticisms of works which he had in fact admired together with don Martín. Inevitably, don Martín was deeply offended. The two parted company, causing enormous pain to don Martín, less perhaps to Lorca who was enjoying some success with his new book.

By 1919, at the age of twenty, Lorca had left Granada for Madrid without having taken his degree at the university, feeling guilty about his quarrel with Berrueta, but by now becoming well-known as a writer of promise. When don Martín died in 1920 Lorca was filled with remorse, and in all his correspondence at that time he had nothing but praise for his old friend, recognizing how much he had learnt from him.

Lorca's artistic personality was formed in Andalusia. From Fuente Vaqueros he took the themes for his early books of poetry and the three rural tragedies; many of these themes were to appear constantly in his drawings as well. In Granada he had begun to refine his aesthetic judgement, and it was there that he made the all-important decision not to become a musician, but to become a writer and a poet instead. He had also begun his career as a draughtsman, which he was never to give up.

DRAWINGS CONCERNED
WITH PERSONAL IDENTITY

His coloured pencils were
his constant companions; with them he
dedicatedly illustrated his works.

Antonina Rodrigo (biographer)

The Residencia de Estudiantes was an educational centre in Madrid, run by Alberto Jimenez Fraud. He had previously worked for three years at the Institución Libre de Enseñanza with Francisco Giner de los Ríos, whose main preoccupation was to create new leaders for Spanish society. Giner was convinced that the only way forward for Spain, both intellectually and economically, was to create a small minority of civilized and dedicated men and women, who would show the way to the rest of the country. These ideas had a profound effect on Jimenez Fraud, who also spent some months in England looking at the English collegiate system. In 1910 Giner de los Ríos invited Jimenez Fraud, then twenty-seven years old, to take charge of an experimental residential educational centre that was to be opened in Madrid. Jimenez Fraud accepted with enthusiasm.

It was to this establishment that Lorca went in 1919, encouraged by his friendship with Fernando de los Ríos, who was related to Francisco Giner de los Ríos and had studied with him at the original Institución Libre de Enseñanza.

Many of Lorca's friends from the Rinconcillo had already moved to Madrid, and they too urged him to come to the capital. However, Lorca did not follow any particular course of studies in Madrid. He continued to be registered at Granada University, and periodically returned there to take exams in an effort to obtain a degree and please his parents.

One of the most innovatory aspects of the Residencia was that it offered residential accommodation to the students so that they could influence each other as well as receive official instruction from teachers. 'The Resi', as it was called, sought to broaden the students' outlook, attempting to

c2 *Paseo de una carpa por un cualto* (Carp wandering about a room)

C3 *Bailarina española* (Spanish dancer)

C4 Soledad Montoya (from *Romance de la pena negra* in *Romancero gitano*)

14 *Querido Melchorito*

bridge the gap between the two cultures, science and art, and to get away from excessive specialization. Emphasis was also placed on the importance of taking responsibility for one's actions and the need for communal effort.

In Lorca's time there were about 150 students at the Resi. Though quite small by modern standards, it was an ideal size for students to get to know each other well. Many of them were medical students, attracted by the excellent new laboratories. The buildings were simply furnished; cleanlines and tidiness were encouraged at all times. Lorca once dropped a cigarette butt on the floor and Jimenez Fraud himself bent down to pick it up, to Lorca's considerable embarrassment. From the start the Resi counted on the support of many distinguished Spaniards, among them Miguel de Unamuno, philosopher and novelist, Chair of Classical Studies at Salamanca; José Ortega y Gasset, philosopher and writer; and Juan Ramón Jimenez, a distinguished poet who later won the Nobel Prize.

Lorca had many friends there, some of whom, such as Salvador Dalí, have become internationally famous. Luis Buñuel, the son of a wealthy solicitor from Zaragoza, who later became a brilliant film director, arrived at the Resi in 1917. There were similarities in Buñuel's and Lorca's backgrounds: both had wealthy fathers and younger mothers who indulged them, and both had wanted to study music in Paris but had been discouraged by their parents. But Buñuel was more disoriented than Lorca, with as yet no real sense of direction, nor a clear idea of what he wanted to study. He changed courses several times, starting with agronomy, switching to engineering, and finally becoming absorbed in entomology. He eventually took a degree in history.

Buñuel's personality developed considerably at the Resi. He became interested in jazz and used to hold 'sessions', listening to records and drinking rum, which was against the rules. He would visit the brothels of Madrid, and was attracted by anarchism. He was also very physical and sportive, apparently jogging barefoot every day even in freezing weather, and he liked to play practical jokes on people such as dousing them with cold water. Buñuel could not fully understand Lorca's latent homosexuality. It was not yet fully acknowledged, probably not even by Lorca himself; and Spanish society at that time was intolerant of such proclivities. Yet even Buñuel admitted that Lorca was in no way effeminate or affected, that the only indication of his homosexuality was that he was not obsessed with women, as most of the other young men were; and this characteristic was usually attributed to his passionate interest in his work.

In truth, perhaps his art and the world of the imagination were sometimes a sublimation of other drives. In Lorca's world sexual symbolism and the images of artistic creativity are often fused, as in the drawing of the several hands (15). Lorca believed that hands are the agents for caresses and sexual activity; they are also indispensable for writing, drawing and playing the piano; therefore, without hands an artist cannot express himself, either sexually or creatively. Very early in Lorca's written

C5 Woman with spotted mantilla

c6 Young man with fish and crook

c7 Young man with crook

work we find hands identified with sexual feelings, possibly illicit ones:

> You were pink
> and then you turned lemon.
>
> What intent did you see in my hand
> which almost threatened you?
>
> I wanted the green apples
> not the pink ones . . .
>
> (OC 398)

In his later work the hand becomes fundamental to life:

> and men's hands have no other purpose than to
> imitate the roots beneath the earth
>
> (OC 459)

The severed hands in the drawing are dripping blood and have roots of their own. In *Divan del Tamarit* Lorca dedicates a whole poem to a hand:

> I don't want to be more than a hand
> a wounded hand, if possible
> I don't want to be more than a hand
> even if I spend a thousand nights without a bed.
>
> (*Casida de la mano imposible*, OC 572)

His drawings often contain images which reappear as leitmotifs throughout his written work.

While he was at the Resi, Lorca became interested in stylistic experiment, the next stage in his development that was to grow upon the solid foundation of his Andalusian background. The students formed many small circles where they discussed modern art, not very seriously – which of course made it more fun. One of the current 'fads' was to invent *anaglifos* – four-line poems in which the last line had to jar completely with the first three, a sort of metric joke. Since rhythm superseded sense, the images became fantastic, involuntarily creating a surreal picture. Predict-

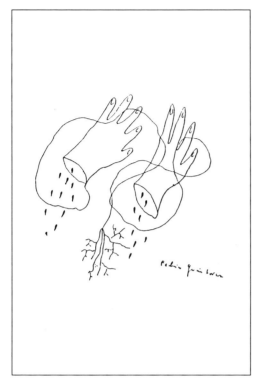

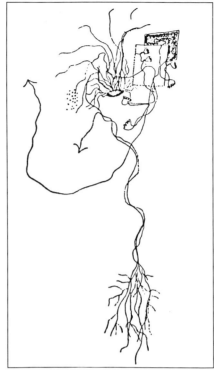

15 Severed hands

16 The eye

ably, Lorca was very good at this game. Another craze was to spot *putre-factos* (putrid ones), the student's name for boring bourgeois people who understood nothing about art or life. Salvador Dalí was particularly good at drawing *putrefactos*, and he and Lorca planned to publish a book of them, with poems by Lorca and drawings by Dalí.

Luis Buñuel founded a society called the Order of Toledo, a homage to that wonderful city he admired so much. He invented all sorts of old-fashioned ranks for the members of his group and stipulated that if some-one wanted to achieve the order of knighthood he had slavishly to admire Toledo, get drunk for at least one night and wander about its streets. Those who went to bed early could only become shield-bearers. Often the members of the Order would wear fancy dress for their gatherings.

c8 Young man with mandolin

c9 Young girl with ruff collar

While enjoying the stimulating antics of the Resi, Lorca was also struggling with his literary career. In 1919 after his initial visit to Madrid he returned to Granada and attended a celebration in honour of his great friend and mentor Fernando de los Ríos, the ex-president of the Artistic Centre of Granada who was now entering the world of politics. The gathering took place in the gardens of the Generalife where, together with other young writers of the day, Lorca read out some of his poems. This was an important event for him because in the audience were Gregorio Martínez Sierra, the director of the most avant-garde theatre in Madrid, the Teatro Eslava, and Catalina Bárcena, a very talented actress and Sierra's girlfriend.

Although Lorca did not recite anything sensational on that occasion, he met Sierra and Bárcena later, at their request, for a further reading in the Alhambra, when he read a poem about a beautiful butterfly which is wounded and falls into a nest of cockroaches; they nurse her to health and a young cockroach falls in love with her, but when her wings have healed she flies off, leaving her young suitor heartbroken. By the end of the poem Catalina Bárcena was in tears. Martínez Sierra promised to stage the story if Lorca could convert it into a play. At this stage of his life Lorca was unsure in which direction to develop his talents, and unwittingly Martínez Sierra was launching him on his career as a dramatist.

Lorca went back to Madrid to try to write the play. There were many delays and changes of title. In the end the title *El maleficio de la Mariposa* (The Butterfly's Spell) was probably arrived at by Martínez Sierra, because, as Federico's brother Francisco has pointed out, *maleficio* was not a word in Federico's vocabulary. The opening night of the play was postponed several times, the costumes and the sets were changed again and again; finally Martínez Sierra put an end to the discussions and the play was staged. It was not well received. The public made sarcastic remarks, some calling for pesticide, and it ran for only four nights. The critics generally agreed that Lorca was a great poet but not a great dramatist, and that the tone of the play was too lyrical. Biographically, it is interesting to speculate on the extent of his identification with Curianito, the jilted lover. At this time he felt very much that love was passing him by and that others were experiencing affection that he somehow lacked.

Lorca pretended not to care about the crass public reaction to his play.

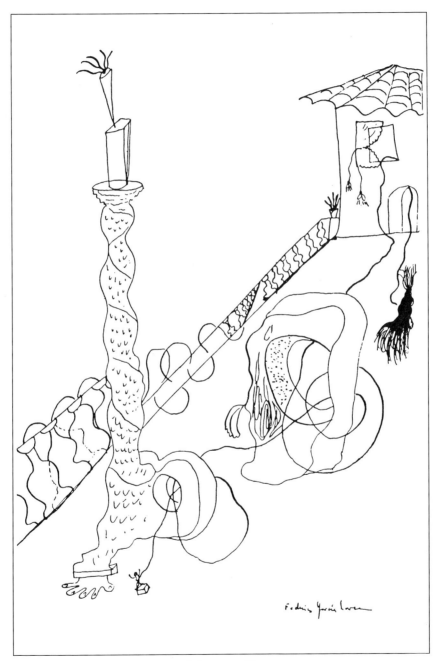

17 Column and house

c10 Virgin of the Seven Swords

CII Young man

On the evening of the first night he went to meet his friends at a well-known café in the calle de Alcalá and laughed aloud about the uproar that his play had created. But in years to come he often pretended that *Mariana Pineda*, written later, was his first play, ignoring the earlier work.

Lorca was experiencing some pressure from his family because he still had no degree of any sort. He returned to Granada to sit exams for his arts degree in the summer of 1920. He passed his research project with flying colours and also passed world history, but failed abysmally on the history of the Spanish language. This distressed his father who badly wanted his eldest son to earn his own living in a profession, rather than messing about with the arts. Lorca's published works so far were not successful, although everyone agreed that he was talented and charming.

Manuel de Falla, the composer and pianist, had recently come to live in Granada. He was about twenty years older than Lorca and not a native of Granada, but he was fascinated by Andalusian song and had wanted for many years to live there. He recalled that in 1920 a young man gave him a conducted tour around the poor quarters of El Albaicín and the Sacro Monte, to help him collect oral ballads from the gypsies. The young man was Lorca. Manuel de Falla and other artists in Granada subsequently planned a song contest for the *cante jondo*, the traditional music of the gypsies, in order to gather them all together and try to annotate some of the music, which was usually not written down because the songs were often improvised. It is not clear whose idea it was but Manuel de Falla and all the organizers, including Lorca, were enthusiastic about it. A petition was drafted and presented to the Council of Granada, who approved the idea. The contest was to be held on 13 and 14 June 1922.

Lorca was inspired to write poems for this competition. He was clearly fascinated by the notions that make up the *cante jondo*: an underlying sadness or *pena*, a close communion with nature, and the sense of cross-cultural influences which go back to the roots of Andalusian identity and in which oriental, gypsy, even Jewish characteristics can be traced.

On the evening of the competition about 4,000 people filled the Plaza de los Aljibes in the Alhambra. The atmosphere was electric. The women wore period flamenco dress with long skirts, and high combs in their hair. The standard of singing was excellent and people came from far and wide to compete.

Lorca's involvement with the organization of this event stimulated him to think about his Andalusian origins and the nature of gypsy song, and to rediscover his lifelong connection with the gypsy people whom he had known since his childhood in Fuente Vaqueros. Thereafter the gypsies became for Lorca a symbol of Andalusia, and there is no doubt that the whole experience of the *cante jondo* contest provided the seed for his famous *Romancero gitano* yet to come. In the poem *Romance de la pena negra* he echoes the *cante jondo* notion of *pena*, and the protagonist, Soledad Montoya, is represented in a drawing (c4). Her anguish and grief are clearly visible.

> Soledad, whom do you seek
> alone and at this hour?
> Whoever it may be
> tell me: what do you care?
> I come to find what I must,
> my joy and my identity.
>
> (OC 436)

Lorca and Falla had planned another project, to revive the traditional puppet theatre of Andalusia, *Los títeres de Cachiporra*, and to travel with it around the mountain villages of the Alpujarra. For this Lorca began in 1922 to write *Tragicomedia de don Cristóbal y la seña Rosita*. Alas, the project never materialized. Instead, he and Falla undertook a simpler production, a performance of some puppet shows for an audience of children in the Lorca home in the Acera del Casino, to which the family had moved in 1917. Falla was in charge of the music, which included Stravinsky, Debussy and Ravel; Lorca wrote some of the playlets and, more interesting in this context, he also made the background sets. The event took place on 5 January 1923, the eve of Epiphany which is celebrated in Spain as the Feast of the Three Kings, who process through the streets distributing gifts to children; another indication of Lorca's keen interest in sustaining Andalusian traditions.

Towards the end of January 1923 Lorca finished his law studies and succeeded in gaining a degree in this subject, spurred on, perhaps, by his desire to please his father and also to be granted permission to travel. He had ambitions to reach Italy.

C12 *Leyenda de Jerez* (Jerez story)

C13 Landscape with red horse

From his balcony in the Acera del Casino, Lorca could see the statue of Mariana Pineda, a local heroine who, according to tradition, had embroidered a flag for her revolutionary lover and then, rather than betray him, had died for the cause of freedom, or love. There are many drawings associated with Mariana (12, 13, 56, 57, 60, C21). Lorca revealed that he was writing a play about her. Martínez Sierra promised to stage it. Although the play was not produced until 1927, it proved to be his first box-office success.

In the summer of 1924 Lorca began writing some of the poems which were eventually published in 1928 as *Romancero gitano*, and he conceived the plot for *La zapatera prodigiosa* (The Shoemaker's Wife), another play which became extremely popular. It tells the story of an older man, a cobbler, who marries a young girl. The marriage is a failure because she feels frustrated. The cobbler then leaves home and returns in the guise of an entertainer. He woos his wife and she duly falls in love with him, but when he removes his mask, the quarrelling starts all over again. There is much well-loved Andalusian tradition in this play, as well as a certain psychological astuteness in the observation that love is in the mind. Two very Lorquian themes are introduced here: the older man unable to satisfy the younger woman, and the idea that he can only cope with reality from behind a mask.

Lorca's friendship with Salvador Dalí, which began at the Resi, was an attraction of opposites. Dalí arrived later than Buñuel and Lorca, in 1923. He was in the middle of his cubist phase. He avoided sentiments and feelings, and hated religion, all of which Lorca valued. But Dalí recognized Lorca's talent and extraordinary personality, and Lorca was able to penetrate Dalí's extreme shyness, which was very pronounced in those days; the exhibitionist tendencies that Dalí developed in later years were a way of overcoming this shyness. Dalí and Lorca had much to talk about, and frequently stayed up until the small hours, arguing and exchanging views. They both came from regions of Spain with a pronounced local culture, but Dalí's Catalonia was more cosmopolitan than Lorca's Andalusia and Dalí was already quite intellectually sophisticated when he arrived at the Resi. His reading included Freud's *Interpretation of Dreams*.

18 Face with arrows   19 Face with arrows

When Lorca was asked to give a talk at the Ateneo in Barcelona, Dalí, on hearing of his friend's impending visit to Catalonia, invited him to spend Holy Week of 1925 with his family at Figueras and Cadaques. Dalí's mother had died in 1920, and he lived with his father and his sister who was then aged seventeen. The Dalís' house at Cadaques, in an idyllic setting by the sea, delighted Lorca and the friendship blossomed. Dalí encouraged Lorca to read his play *Mariana Pineda* to the assembled family. The theme appealed to the liberal-minded Catalans, and they were all extremely moved by it; thereafter Dalí's father treated Federico like a second son. Although the play had been verbally accepted for production, Martínez Sierra had then changed his mind, possibly fearing some disciplinary measure from the right-wing dictatorship of Primo de Rivera.

The trip to Catalonia was to prove a turning point in Lorca's life. There is little doubt that he was in love with Dalí, a fact which Dalí confirmed, although he claimed that he never responded to Lorca's advances. After the visit they kept up a lengthy correspondence. Dalí enjoyed Lorca's letters, reading them over and over again for the richness of their imagery.

C14 Clown

C15 Word play with red horse

20 Greetings for a Saint's Day

This he readily admitted to Lorca, often praising him for his work and even alluding to his good looks. It seems likely that Dalí was also very much infatuated with Lorca but that he suppressed his own homosexual inclinations more than his friend did. According to Dalí, Lorca had to vent his passion on an unknown girl, the first woman he ever slept with.

From this time Lorca's love stories became sadder, with more emphasis on the mask theme. The mask objectively represented the split between his social self and the solitude which lay behind. His infatuation with Dalí must have confirmed to him where his real inclinations lay; this was a problem to a young Spaniard in the 1920s. His writing became more experimental, more universal, influenced by Dalí and the Catalan artists he had met. In the summer of 1925 he began to write a short playlet which was eventually published as *El paseo de Buster Keaton* (Buster Keaton's Walk). Buster Keaton is the tragic clown, the sensitive humorist who is misunderstood. Lorca describes Keaton's eyes in the stage directions:

> His eyes, infinite and sad, like those of a new-born animal, dream of lilies, angels, and satin sashes. His eyes which are like the bottom of a glass. The eyes of an idiot child. Which are hideous. Which are gorgeous. His ostrich eyes. His human eyes, securely balanced on melancholia.
>
> (OC 894)

21 Falling mask

Could these be Dalí's eyes? Lorca's feelings infused? We do not know. The appeal of the clown figure, the costumed buffoon, is a by-product of the mask theme, the disguise we must wear to face the world. There are many Lorca drawings of clowns, most of them sad, some wearing a mask which is seen falling to one side to reveal a different expression behind it (21, 22, C14).

22 Clown mask

23 Love

24 *La mujer del abanico*
(Woman with fan)

The questions of identity and reality become ever more fascinating. Another attraction for Lorca is that of the harlequin, a creature who can contain conflicting emotions simultaneously. The shifting colours referred to in an early poem called *Arlequín* describe the harlequin's multi-faceted personality, his ability to see into all realities and understand all varieties of sexual experience:

> Red Breast of the sun
> Blue breast of the moon
> Torso half coral
> Half silver and shadow
>
> (OC 367)

The sun is a male symbol and the moon a female symbol; clearly the harlequin represents the bisexual dilemma. He also stands for the conflict

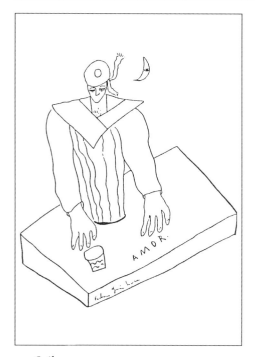

25 Sailor   26 Sailor

between mind and body, with blue and silver representing the mind while red and coral represent the body. The dilemma is expressed through visual imagery.

The sailor is another visual symbol through which Lorca explores the question of identity. Here again, as with the severed hands, sexual freedom is identified with the notion of creative freedom. The sailor has much in common with the gypsy in that they are both outside society and to a certain extent they both represent freedom and the natural life. But the sailor seems to be further removed from society than the gypsy: he is an exile by choice rather than by birth. In the drawings (23, 25, 26, 27, 28) he is sometimes associated with love or is represented with wings, able to fly. The word 'love' is often written on a drawing of a sailor, and sometimes there is an inviting bedroom in the background. The inference seems to be that if one has love, one is free. But the sailor's

27 Sailor

28 Sailor

love is always anticipatory. He seems to be a symbol of, rather than a participant in, life. We never see the sailor engaged in activity: his life is an abstraction, not a reality.

The sailor as the object of another's love represents an unattainable ideal. The theme of the frustration of love can be seen most clearly in the play *Así que pasen cinco años* (Five Years Go By), written in 1931. The protagonist, a poet, is waiting for his fiancée to return. When she does, she falls in love with another more virile character; a typical Lorquian anxiety. As the play ends we discover that all the action has taken place in the mind of the poet – nothing has really happened. The play is surreal, questioning our conventional notions of reality. Nearly all the characters have an imaginative counterpart on another level of reality. The harlequin tells the girl that her love is to be found:

> Half-way round
> the wind and the sea
>
> (OC 1110)

The girl is frightened and says,

> You won't give him to me
> One can never reach
> the bottom of the sea
>
> (OC 1110)

This is the kind of love that the sailor is associated with. He is the only character in Lorca's world who symbolizes love in the way it should be but never actually is; he lives in a dream-world of constant expectation. In the play, the tone of the girl's words is both happy and sad. Initially she is overjoyed at knowing where her love is – she has found him, her ideal. She has a fantasy of what her love should be, but characteristically this love is difficult to reach; her love is at 'the bottom of the sea'. After a brief repartee with the harlequin, who is aware of the impossibility of her love, she becomes 'frightened of reality' and exits, crying.

There are more references to sailors in the drawings than in the writing. They are sometimes portrayed drunk, or entombed from the waist downward, which seems to suggest that passion leads to death and destruction

– another typically Lorquian theme, developed for example in his play *Bodas de Sangre* in which the bride, who elopes with her true love on the very day of her marriage to another, is frustrated in the end because the two men kill each other. One drawing of a sailor bears the caption, 'Only mystery keeps us alive, only mystery' (27). The inference seems to be that love is best when confined to the mind. In a short playlet called *La doncella, el marinero y el estudiante* (The Young Girl, the Sailor and the Student, 1925) the sailor is overtly sexually flirtatious in his approach to the girl. He asks to see her thighs. But his pursuit goes no further and he retires into a corner to play an 'accordion as dusty and tired as the seventeenth century'. (OC 900)

Another feature of the sailor drawings is that flowers grow out of the eyes (27, 28). In the poetry there are many references to flowers coming out of the mouth, as in:

> We shall see our shining ring, and roses
> flowering from our mouths.
>
> (OC 493)

and:

> Oh my ancient voice of love
> . . . . .
> when all roses flowered from my tongue
>
> (OC 498)

When flowers grow out of facial features Lorca is describing a state of intense happiness and fulfilment, usually associated with an imaginary time in the future, or a long-lost paradise in the past. The sailor's eyes, without pupils, empty except for flowers, suggest this dream-like frame of mind.

From these less Andalusian works we can see that Lorca was profoundly influenced by Dalí, both artistically and personally – if the two can be separated. Lorca absorbed and emulated Dalí's desire for order and almost mathematical objectivity in composition. This approach, breaking away both from a mirror-like reproduction of reality and from the woolly-

29 Salvador Dalí

mindedness of impressionism, is expressed in his famous *Oda a Salvador Dalí* (1926) where he describes something like the birth of cubism:

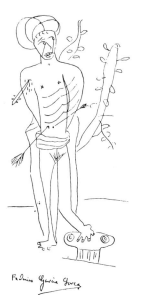

Sailors who know nothing of wine at dusk
are decapitating mermaids in the seas of lead.
And Night, black statue of Prudence,
holds in her hand the round mirror of the moon.

We are overcome by a longing for shape and outline.
The man with the yellow yardstick is coming,
Venus is a still-life in white
and the butterfly collectors are fleeing.

(OC 619)

30 San Sebastián

The most moving part of the poem is the passage in praise of friendship, which states that he and Dalí would always value love and human experience above art. The lines on Dalí himself reveal Dalí's satisfaction in his work, that he knows exactly what he is doing:

Oh Salvador Dalí of the olive voice!
I do not praise your imperfect adolescent brush
nor your colour which haunts the colour of your time,
but I praise your desire for an outlined eternity.

Your hygienic soul lives on new marble.
You flee from the dark jungle of incredible forms.
Your fantasy extends to where your hands reach,
and you enjoy the sonnet of the sea at your window.

(OC 619)

Oda a Salvador Dalí was much commented on by critics since it heralded a style that was new both for Lorca and for other Spanish writers of the time. The influence of cubism is also evident in a number of Lorca's drawings (C12, C16). The double images reveal an interest in varying shapes and textures but also show a concern with shifting aspects of personality. Lorca rarely let go of the human element, except perhaps in no. 17, though even here the basis of the drawing is human, a visual joke. The balancing

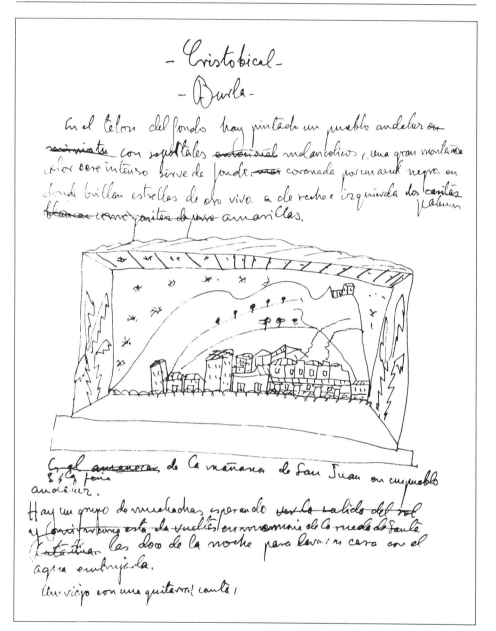

31 Drawing for a puppet set

act of the column on a hand, with a carrot at the top, is very Daliesque, as are the hollow objects, which are reminiscent of Dalí's *apparells* (things).

Early in 1926 The Artistic Centre of Granada died out through lack of interest and was replaced by the new Ateneo Científico, Literario y Artístico. Lorca was chosen to give the inaugural lecture. He spoke about *La imágen poética de don Luis de Góngora*, and naturally enough his assessment of the great seventeenth-century poet reflected his own tastes. He praised Góngora for the limitations that he imposed on himself, for the way in which he did not let his imagination run wild; and he referred to Góngora's ability to bring together the cosmic and the minute, which is of course a characteristic of Lorca's own work. In his talk, Lorca also stated that 'no-one who is born blind can be a plastic poet of objective images'. (oc 68)

In the summer of 1926 Dalí went to Madrid intending to make a final break with his art school. His plan was to go back to Figueras and paint furiously for a year, then go to Paris with all his new work and take the city by storm. At this time Lorca and Dalí must have seen each other every day, and Lorca missed Dalí a lot when they separated. Lorca's career was not going so well. His parents constantly alluded to the success of his younger brother Francisco who was a model student, doing postgraduate work at Oxford. By now Lorca had written two plays, *La zapatera prodigiosa* and *Mariana Pineda*. He felt sure that the latter especially would be a box-office success and would get him out of financial difficulty and total dependence on his parents, but he could get neither of them produced.

Towards the end of 1926 Lorca became rather depressed. He considered becoming a teacher but did not really know how to go about it. He talked about buying himself a filing cabinet but he didn't really know what to file. He talked about getting married, the need to settle down, put down some roots. He had three books of poems which he wanted to publish: *Suites, Poema del cante jondo* and *Canciones*. He badly needed some public recognition.

THREE

EXPERIMENTAL DRAWINGS

**If it were not for you, the Catalans,
I would not have continued drawing.**

F. G. Lorca

Early in 1927, Lorca and his fellow writers conceived the idea of creating a literary supplement to *El Defensor de Granada*, one of the principal newspapers of Granada. They would call it *gallo* (cock), or *gallo del Defensor*. Lorca asked his old friends to make contributions. One of the members of the Rinconcillo, Melchor Fernández Almagro, now a successful journalist in Madrid writing theatre reviews, was asked to write something, as was Dalí. Dalí was now enjoying considerable success. Four of the paintings he was exhibiting at the Galerías Dalmau in Barcelona in January 1927 represented the head of Lorca, and Dalí readily admitted that he was very much involved with Lorca's personality at this time; but he was critical of his plans for *gallo*. The idea of publishing a literary magazine was too conventional for Dalí, a completely unadventurous move. Nevertheless, the first edition of *gallo* in 1928 did contain work by Dalí: drawings and a prose poem called *San Sebastián*, translated from the Catalan. Dalí and Lorca were both fascinated by Saint Sebastian. The subject was an intimate point of contact between them. The image they had in mind was probably a reproduction of Mantegna's beautiful young man pierced through with arrows, his eyes turned heavenward. Lorca did a rough sketch of Saint Sebastian (30).

Throughout this time he was becoming increasingly anxious about the production of *Mariana Pineda*. He wanted Margarita Xirgu, the leading Catalan actress, to perform it, but there were hitches. When she finally agreed, Lorca began to worry about the play being dated. His work had developed substantially since he had written it, and he felt under constant pressure from Dalí to experiment and eschew tradition.

It was finally decided that *Mariana Pineda* would open in Barcelona.

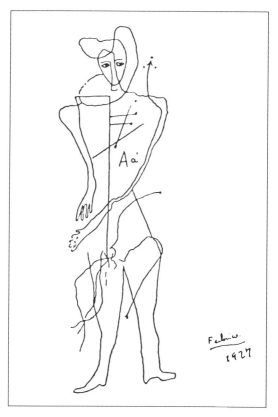

32 Figure

Lorca was happy at the prospect of seeing Dalí again and must have written to him suggesting that he take charge of the sets because Dalí wrote back describing how he visualized them. Lorca was thrilled; Dalí's sets completely captured the flavour of Andalusia (although Dalí had never been there), and were designed in such a way that the scenery was much smaller than the proscenium arch, giving the impression of a set within a set. Lorca wanted his scenes to be viewed like a series of friezes or etchings, and the designs emphasized this two-dimensional quality. The first night of *Mariana Pineda* took place on 24 June 1927 and was an enormous success, the audience clamouring for Lorca and Margarita Xirgu at the end of every act. The critics agreed unanimously that Lorca was on the road to success.

Perhaps it was the elation of the first night which gave him the confidence to show his drawings to a well-known art critic in Barcelona, Sebastián Gasch. After some discussion, plans were made to exhibit Lorca's drawings at the Galerías Dalmau while *Mariana Pineda* was on at the Teatro Goya. The Galerías Dalmau was the leading modern art gallery in Barcelona, and possibly the most important centre for the dissemination of modern art in Spain, so it was a great honour to be exhibited there.

The first one-man exhibition consisted of twenty-four drawings:

1. Claro de luna	Moonlight
2. Sueño del marino	Sailor's dream
3. Vaso de cristal	Crystal vase
4. Vaso de cristal	Crystal vase
5. Dama en el balcón	Lady on the balcony (4)
6. Payaso	Clown
7. Gota de agua	Drop of water
8. Ojo de pez	Fish eye
9. Escándalo	Scandal
10. Santa Teresa del Santísimo Sacramento	Saint Teresa of the Holy Sacrament
11. Claro de circo	Circus ring
12. Naturaleza muerta	Still life
13. Payaso japonés	Japanese clown
14. Leyenda de jerez	Jerez story (C12)
15. Teorema del jarro	Theorem of the jar
16. La mantilla	The mantilla (possibly 5)
17. La musa de Berlín	Berlin muse (34)
18. El viento este	East wind
19. Teorema de la copa y de la mandolina	Theorem of the glass and the mandolin (C17)
20. Merienda	Snack (C16)
21. Pecera	Fishtank (possibly C19)
22. Beso en el espejo	Mirror kiss

23. Naturaleza muerta	Still life (C18)
24. Retrato de Salvador Dalí	Portrait of Salvador Dali

Unfortunately it is not now possible to identify all these drawings. Many have been dispersed and their whereabouts are not known; others have had their names changed by owners or editors. What is interesting about those we can identify is that they show that Lorca was trying to pull away from his old representational style and experiment with cubist techniques and subject matter. This can be seen most clearly in the drawings numbered 14, 19, 20, 23 in the exhibition list.

The exhibition was shown for only one week, from 25 June to 2 July, and did not arouse much critical attention. However, Sebastián Gasch published an article in *L'Amic de les Arts* in September 1927, which is here translated from the Catalan:

THE ARTS: AN EXHIBITION OF F. G. LORCA

Lorca's drawings at the Dalmau Gallery!

Let the bureaucrats of art, the pigs, the sedentary, pass by!

Let the superficial, the self-sufficient, the responsible people pass along!

Lorca's drawings are directed exclusively at the pure, the simple, those who are capable of feeling without understanding. To those who delight in the infinite poetry of allusive objects, anti-artistic and anti-transcendental, in the illustrated postcard, culminating in the pathetic intensity of the bistro placard.

Concrete poetry invented by Jean Cocteau.

There remains little more to say about these drawings.

Products of pure intuition, it is inspiration that guides the hand of their author. A hand that abandons itself. A hand that lets itself go, that offers no resistance, that does not know or wish to know where it is being led.

This article – more of a manifesto than a critical review – was probably only read in Catalonia. But Dalí also wrote a review of the exhibition in September 1927, which was published in *La Nova Revista*. The first part of it is somewhat obscure and discusses metaphysical theories and cubism in general terms; the second part concentrates on Lorca:

> Lorca's aphrodisiac instinct always precedes his imagination, his spiritual qualities take second place. When occasionally his imagination is more to the forefront, the drawings resent it and are relegated to the realm of simple, more or less delightful illustrations of a popular-naive kind.
>
> The poetic style of Lorca's drawings tends towards an organic absence of matter, expressed in the finest physiological calligraphy. Lorca, who is wholly Andalusian, has an age-old instinct for colour and architectural relationships, which are discharged in an uncontrolled harmonious asymmetry that characterizes all the purest visual art of the east.
>
> In Lorca's best drawings, such as 'Drop of Water', the finest, most exquisite eastern poisons have been introduced, those subtle but deadly poisons that in western art's grim moments of anaemia have suddenly become the elixir of life and eternal youth.
>
> Occasionally, at their best, Lorca's drawings take something from the graphic lines of the surrealists, and from the frivolous and irridescent decoration of the coloured interiors and spirals of glass balls.
>
> These aphrodisiac visual and poetic qualities in Lorca's recently exhibited drawings have, however, in my opinion, just one defect, a fault which it is unlikely the Catalans will ever have: the defect, every day more irresistible, of extreme preciousness.

Although much of this is difficult to follow, it seems that Dalí is being uncomplimentary about his friend's drawings; and from about this time onward his attitude to Lorca is ambivalent. Although he always claimed that he refused Lorca's advances, there is little doubt that he was now just as obsessed with Lorca as Lorca had been with him in the preceding two years. Two Dalí drawings published in 1927 contain references to Lorca: *La playa* (The beach) (*Verso y Prosa*, Murcia 1927) and *Federico en la playa de Ampurias* (Federico on the beach at Ampurias) (*L'Amic de les Arts*, Sitges 1927). (The second is referred to by Lorca on a postcard

33 Figure

34 *La musa de Berlín* (The Berlin Muse)

to Dalí in May 1927, so he must have seen it before it was published.)
Two paintings by Dalí, also made in 1927, contain representations of
Lorca's head: *La miel es mas dulce que la sangre* (Honey is sweeter than
blood), and *Los esfuerzos estériles* (Fruitless effort).

But although this shows Dalí's interest in Lorca, there is, of course,
no reason to assume that he liked Lorca's drawings. In 1927 their friendship was at its most intense. After that summer the two men grew further
apart, either for artistic or personal reasons.

Towards the end of the summer Lorca and his family went to the seaside
resort of Lanjarón where Federico was possessed by a feverish burst of
creativity that led him mainly to draw. The Catalan art critic Sebastián
Gasch continued to take a lively interest in Lorca's graphic work, and
together they planned to publish a book of the drawings. Lorca's reply
to one of Sebastián's Gasch's letters is worth quoting, since it seems to

35 Two figures

36 *Arlequín veneciano* (Venetian
     harlequin)

suggest his drawing had surrealist characteristics, although the word surrealism is carefully never mentioned:

> I am grateful to you for your praise; you have no idea how this helps me
> to draw and I really derive pleasure from drawing. First I give myself a
> subject before drawing – and then I achieve the same effect as when I don't
> think of anything at all. Certainly in these moments I find that I experience
> an almost physical sensibility which carries me to places where it is difficult
> to remain standing on one's feet, where one is almost flying over the abyss.
> It requires effort: hopeless to sustain a normal conversation with these
> people at the seaside resort of Lanjarón, because my eyes and my words
> are elsewhere. They are in the enormous library which nobody has ever
> read, in the coolest of atmospheres, a country where things dance on one
> leg.

> (OC 1658)

It is clear that Lorca attached importance to his graphic work, and that he felt he was truly experimenting and developing through his drawing. Gasch must have spoken to him about the dangers of abandoning himself to the unconscious, for in another letter to Gasch in which he encloses some drawings, he explains that he executes his drawings

> without torture or dreams (I can't stand dream art), or complications. These drawings are simultaneously pure poetry and pure art. I feel myself to be clean, comforted, happy, childlike, when I do them. I am horrified by the painting they call direct, which is no more than an anguished battle with form in which the painter always emerges vanquished and with the work dead ... Moreover, I would call these drawings which you will receive (I am sending them registered) very human drawings. Because nearly all of them strike a little arrow in the heart.
>
> (OC 1659)

Lorca's avoidance of dream images and his firm anchorage in the world of human emotions is perhaps the area in which he is most at odds with Salvador Dalí.

Mariana Pineda was staged in Madrid on 12 October 1927. Lorca himself wrote an article in *ABC* before the play opened, explaining what he was trying to do. He stressed the importance of seeing the play as a series of etchings or visual scenes, and he talked of his nocturnal, lunar and infantile tendencies. The play was a huge success. Most critics dwelt on its two-dimensional visual qualities, but only one, Francisco Ayala, recognized the distancing effect of these scenes or cameos, and how the author strove to achieve a greater objectivity through the use of this technique. His interpretation revealed the play in a much more modern light and Lorca's fears about being old-fashioned and bound by tradition were slightly allayed.

Lorca wrote to Dalí telling him of the success of *Mariana Pineda* in Madrid, using his sets. Dalí was pleased, although he was annoyed with Margarita Xirgu for not paying for the sets. Lorca and Dalí had planned that as soon as Lorca started making money they would bring out an *Anti-Artistic Review*. Dalí detested conventionally 'arty' painting. He did not want people to look at his work with preconceived assumptions; he wanted it to be viewed with naive innocence, with nothing whatsoever

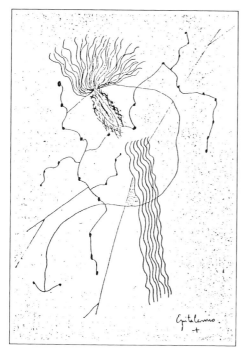

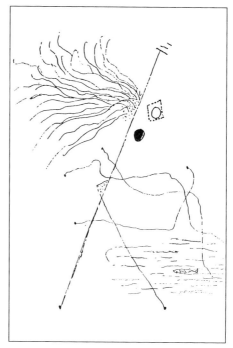

37 *Epitalamio* (Epithalamium)   38 *Sirena* (Mermaid)

remembered of previous works of art. Dalí was veering towards surrealism, although he did not publicly admit it.

Dalí's friendship and influence were of enormous importance in Lorca's development both as writer and artist, encouraging him to think about art and to experiment with new techniques. There would have been no variety of texture in Lorca's drawings, no search for geometric form, without Dalí (C16, C17), and he would not have dared to draw from his innermost feelings and create a strange world of ghostly 'personages' without Dalí (32, 33, 35, 36). Dalí was much more of a rebel than Lorca. He was not concerned with what people thought of his work, caring only about pushing back the confines of art, about challenging all preconceived notions. This was good for Lorca. Dalí encouraged Lorca to express what he felt, not borrowed ideas. From now on, Lorca not only experiments with form but is more identified with his work, talking more about himself.

By 1928 Lorca claimed that he had finished the revision of *La zapatera prodigiosa*. He was preparing *Oda al Santísimo Sacramento* and also a lecture on children's nursery songs. *Romancero gitano* was about to appear, and he wanted to publish some drawings together with Dalí. As usual, he was working on several things at once; nothing seemed too much for his restless energy and vitality.

In March the magazine *gallo* was about to appear in Granada. The young men who produced it with Lorca badly wanted it to shock the bourgeois provincialism of Granada and to that extent they succeeded. There were many references in the magazine to *americana*, a racy, dangerous way of life that was unknown to the *granadinos*. Dalí was upset at the way his *San Sebastián* appeared, although no-one could quite understand why, since it had not been altered or edited.

Two weeks after the appearance of *gallo* the people of Granada were surprised by the advent of yet another literary magazine *Pavo* (Turkey). This magazine seemed to be at odds with the thinking of *gallo*; but after many amusing sallies and verbal jokes, it emerged that *Pavo* was in fact the product of the same team as *gallo*.

gallo was much praised by journals and critics in Granada, as well as by *L'Amic de les Arts* in Catalonia and *La gaceta literaria* in Madrid. Its aim was to reconcile its readers to modern times. Joaquín Amigo, one of the young editors, wrote:

Let us bathe our pupils in the marvellous reality which we have before us; let us attempt to capture the real essence of our time and let us learn to extract its own beauty from it, just as in other eras when people were true to themselves, they knew how to go about it, and so made original creations.

In March 1928 Sebastián Gasch wrote an article about Lorca's drawings in *La gaceta literaria*. He describes Lorca's spontaneity:

A style that is full of abandon, that puts up no resistance, that does not know and does not wish to know which way it is going, a style that paints without effort, without torture, with optimism, with joy, with the joy of a child who covers a wall in doodles . . .

And he likens Lorca to other contemporary artists:

When we look at Lorca's drawings we think of that involuntary style of drawing with which Picasso used to achieve excellent results: see the illustrations to Stravinsky's 'Rag Time'. We also think of the drawings of Miró, who is so alert to the visions of his interior world, which he tranfers quickly onto paper as they present themselves to him, in the same way as the poet writes in his notebook the metaphor which he has just created.

So far Gasch has insisted on the involuntariness of Lorca's drawing, which is perhaps why Lorca was eager to protect himself from the surrealist tag. But this involuntariness is related more to the form of the drawings, the manner in which they are executed, than to their substance. On this question Gasch says:

Lorca's drawings do not imitate nature. Nature is one thing and art another. And art must play a more elevated role than merely copying with abject servility the objects of nature, which are all right as they are, which are already beautiful enough, which cannot be copied. Art must not commit the folly of wishing to imitate the inimitable. The essential thing for the artist is to be found in the clash between his interior world and the exterior world.

This was indeed the new conception of art. The artist was expected to paint what he thought he saw rather than what he actually saw. It was more important to paint a good picture than to represent reality.

Gasch suggests that the artist should represent his own interior world, the visual counterpart of a poetic mythology:

The real artist constructs an interior world, with elements taken from reality, and this nourishes his imagination. An interior world wherein aspects of reality become lodged and classified, not according to an objective logic, but rather according to a subjective order, which is the only one of interest to the artist.

39 Mermaid

He argues that the interior is not pure fantasy because there is no such thing as pure imagination: it must feed on something which is necessarily reality. The imagined world can become as real as the reality which kindled it.

While *gallo* was at the height of its success, Lorca went off to Madrid to stay at the Resi and correct the proofs of *Romancero gitano*. Summer courses were being organized for visiting foreign professors. The Resi was now at its peak, and Lorca was the resident poet. During his absence from Granada, *gallo* collapsed, and his brother Francisco wrote to him chiding him and others for their lack of co-operation on the magazine.

At this time Lorca was involved with a sculptor called Emilio Aladrén, who had been studying at the same school as Dalí. Aladrén came from Zaragoza; he was the son of a military man and was eight years younger than Lorca. By all accounts he was very good-looking, dark, temperamental. Lorca had known him in 1925 but their friendship had not developed until 1927. Aladrén seems to have been an unpleasant character, exploiting Lorca at every turn and using his success to become well known in society. None of Lorca's friends liked him. They all said that he was a terrible sculptor and a person of dubious morality and intelligence who led a chaotic life, and they agreed that he was a bad influence on Lorca. But Federico took him everywhere, introduced him to his friends, and told everyone what a wonderful sculptor he was. In 1928 Aladrén made a sculpture of Federico's head which Lorca tried to promote without success.

The publication of *Romancero gitano* was eagerly anticipated by the literary world. Most people had heard one or two poems by Lorca at various cultural events and had been much impressed; seldom had such a sense of expectancy surrounded a book of poems. Towards the end of July 1928 *Romancero gitano* appeared on the bookstalls, beautifully presented with Lorca's own drawing on the cover (66). The book was highly praised by the critics and sold out quickly. Lorca had become famous.

It was at this time that Lorca read a newspaper article about a young bride in Almería who eloped with her cousin on her wedding day, a story that was to provide the germ for his play *Bodas de sangre*. He actually wrote the play four years later and it was first performed in Madrid in March 1933.

In the summer of 1928 Lorca returned to Granada. Everyone praised his work; but instead of feeling elated by his success, he was plunged into a strange depression. In letters to friends he talked of the 'stupid fame' and the bright lights projected on him from the outside world which were killing his sensitivity and privacy.

Dalí wrote to him, chiding him about what he had done in Madrid, perhaps alluding to his relationship with Aladrén. They discussed the possibility of Dalí going to stay in Granada in the autumn. Lorca was also trying to exorcise his depression by writing *Oda al Santísimo Sacramento* and *Oda a Sesostris*, an unfinished work which had a homosexual theme. As a result of his relationship with Aladrén, he seemed to be in a state of great conflict about his homosexuality. He sent Sebastián Gasch two prose poems, *Nadadora sumergida* (Submerged Swimmer) and *Suicidio en Alejandría* (Suicide in Alexandria), together with two drawings, for publication in *L'Amic de les Arts*. They appeared in September 1928 next to a Dalí text. *Nadadora sumergida* contains a long farewell scene, and the accompanying drawing (35) seems to describe two souls embracing (for the last time?) on a beach; one cannot help feeling that both refer to the estrangement of Dalí and Lorca.

Lorca had learnt much from Dalí and had proved in *Nadadora sumergida* and *Suicido en Alejandría* that he could write in a modern objective style. *Romancero gitano*, however, had revealed his admiration for the traditional Spanish ballad and his nostalgia for familiar Andalusian situations. Dalí disapproved. He felt that Lorca had betrayed all their plans for what constituted the truly poetical, a vivid imaginative evasion of reality. He wrote Lorca a long and critical letter after the publication of *Romancero gitano*, chastising him for reviving a world of commonplace clichés. The worst poem, he said, was the one about the man who took a girl to the river, *La casada infiel* (The Unfaithful Wife). He accused Lorca of moving in a world of accepted realities which were anti-poetical. Dalí's comments on the reference to the horseback rider reveal how far his own understanding of art had moved even from physiological fact:

> . . . you talk of a rider and you suppose he goes above a horse and that
> the horse gallops. This is assuming a great deal, because in fact it would
> be a good thing to verify whether it is the rider who is above or not, whether

the reins are not an organic extension of the very same hands, whether in fact the pubic hairs on the rider's balls are not faster than the horse, and whether the horse is not something immobile adhered to the ground by strong roots . . .

Dalí accuses Lorca of selling out to the *putrefactos* by writing easily intelligible poetry for them.

Lorca must have felt wounded by this letter. Dalí's obvious interest in surrealism, although he always denied its influence, was closer to Buñuel's world than Lorca's. Buñuel had been working for some time in Paris in the film world, and his reaction to *Romancero gitano* was similar to Dalí's. He accused Lorca of 'flamenco drama' and a continuation of 'centuries of classical ballads'.

Meanwhile Lorca remained in Granada, hoping that Dalí might visit him. So much criticism from his old friend could hardly fail to depress him; but the criticism certainly had its effect. On 11 October 1928 he delivered a lecture at the Ateneo in Granada on *Imaginación, inspiración y evasión en la poesía*, incorporating the ideas on evasion which Dalí had insisted on in his letter. Illustration 16 appears to be a graphic account of the creative process as outlined in this talk. The eye is the main organ of communication with the outside world. The nerve lines emanating from the eye relay the messages which it receives to different parts of the body. The lines leading upward to the brain take the perceived reality to the mind where it is converted into 'thought' or abstracted in some way. The lines going down describe the eye's relationship to the body: there the eye's message becomes 'feeling'. There are also two arrows pointing outwards towards reality. One is connected to two reflecting panels near the brain, behind the eye. The two panels, one dark and one light, represent the way reality is changed within the brain. The first panel, the lighter one, is 'imagination' as described in the lecture. The second, darker panel, which is further removed from reality, stands for the poetic imagination, or 'evasion'. The drawing tells us that the information received by the eye is relayed to the brain where it enters the world of the imagination. From there it moves into the world of poetic imagination, whence it will emerge as a work of art; this is symbolized by the minute hands around the two panels, groping for expression.

On 26 October 1928, again at the Ateneo, Lorca gave a talk on modern art called *Sketch de la pintura moderna*. Here too we can see the influence of Dalí. In this lecture (see Appendix A) Lorca shows a remarkable knowledge of modern art. He starts with an invective against impressionism, in which he emphasizes the need for form rather than light. He objects to what he calls *sensacionismo* or *momentismo*: in other words, that impressionism only captures one moment in time; he also attacks the imitation of nature and the suppression of non-objective elements. Lorca is actually criticizing the situation in painting around the 1880s, when the impressionist painters were delighting in the physical world around them. Later, their experiments with light and colour did in fact become much more systematized, in the hands of such artists as Seurat, Gauguin and van Gogh. This cerebralism – or *control inteligente* – led more naturally into cubism, which is what Lorca approves of. In this progression away from the old system of reference Lorca is aware that the boundaries between mathematics and art are no longer clearly defined. The surrealist and dada manifestations of an awareness of a new reality were not expressed intellectually (as the cubists, constructivists and purists had attempted to do), but imaginatively. It is this liberation of the artist's mind from a conventional view of nature that Lorca favours in surrealism, although he finds the dadaists somewhat frivolous and undisciplined.

Lorca goes on to discuss the effect on art of the First World War and how its enormous impact changed people's concept of reality and the artist's portrayal of it. The influence of the war as a generating force in modern art is especially true of surrealism, which began as a philosophy of life, a reaction to the horror of war, rather than an aesthetic movement.

Lorca admires Juan Gris and hails him as the master of pure material, form and colour. He also acknowledges Picasso and Georges Braque as the leaders of the wartime generation. But he does not favour art with a message, as he believes futurism to be. Lorca's remarks about futurism are very perceptive, given that he is making these comments in 1928 when the spirit of revolution in art was still strong. He claims that, with the arrival of the cinema, there is no justification for futurism. He also condemns Marinetti for joining the fascist movement under Mussolini. He admires the work of Miró, saying that Miró has *duende* (inspiration, literally 'a gnome', rather like a leprechaun).

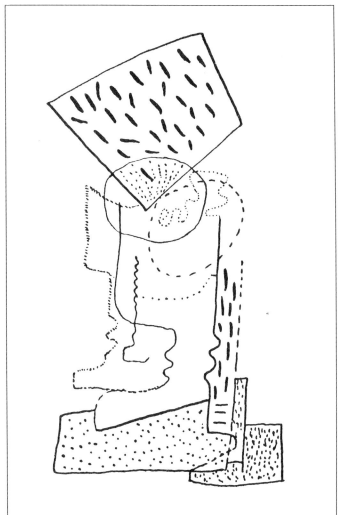

40 Composition

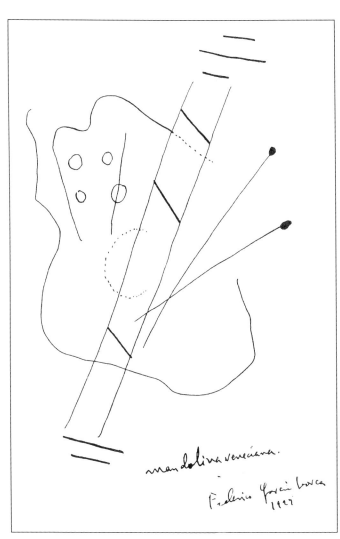

41 *Mandolina veneciana* (Venetian mandolin)

42 Music and mask

Lorca's debt to Miró in his own drawings is noticeable in his repeated representation of the moon and small objects. Possibly he was consciously or unconsciously emulating Miró, for the reasons that he gives in his lecture.

In the 1920s Miró was beginning to be associated with the surrealists although he never participated in their group activities. Breton declared him to be on the right path, but Miró did not care whether or not this was so. The rigid automatism advocated by Breton was a poor imitation of the call of real inspiration. The period of Miró's work which probably had most effect on Lorca was from 1923–7 when Miró was at a turning point in his artistic expression, oscillating between realistic representation and abstraction. Later, in the 1940s, Miró was to try to invent a symbolic language to describe his interior world, but this would have been of less value for someone like Lorca, who never reached such a complete stage of abstraction.

Both Miró and Lorca rejected formal surrealism as an artistic movement yet at the same time both advocated spontaneity and creative freedom, which made them very acceptable to the surrealists.

The art critic Jacques Dupin's assessment of Miró's drawings could easily be applied to Lorca's, (especially 32, 33, 35, 36, 43):

> It often happens that a figure or 'personage' emerges from the progression of his line, from the effusion of his spots, or an animal appears among the ambiguous shapes and enigmatic signs. Miró created many of these 'personages' but they are always the same uncertain, ghostly white, with a fluctuating sinuous contour, the only parts insistently developed are the head, the foot, the genitals or the eye. These 'personages' are devoid of all materiality, all corporeal density.
>
> (Dupin 162)

Another Miró device which Lorca practised was the introduction of words or letters into his pictures (26, C3, C15). As Dupin says:

> By introducing, or rather by integrating words or phrases in his pictures, Miró produced a number of what he calls his 'picture-poems'.
>
> (Dupin 164)

A characteristic common to both artists which cannot be overlooked is the eroticism of their drawings. Even in the most abstract of Lorca's drawings, the repeated representation of arrows suggests a preoccupation with phallic symbols. Certain themes in Lorca's poetry and drawings are also reminiscent of Miró, for example the concentration on eyes as an important sensory medium, hands and feet as means of expression (15, 16, 17, C13), the emphasis on genitalia. But Miró is essentially an abstract thinker, a rarifier of reality. He therefore appeals to Lorca's philosophical, universal outlook.

Juan Gris provides a useful point of departure for a study of Lorca's concrete imagery. Gris was also interested in breaking down the barriers between the arts. It is surely from Gris that Lorca derives his concern for cubist technique in drawing (as in 41, C16, C17, C18, C19). Gris was primarily interested in the object and wanted to represent it as fully as possible. He would record the object's colour – sometimes only in part, leaving the viewer to fill in the remaining areas – and also its surface, which he would treat according to his personal response to its texture – wood, cloth, stone, etc. This variety of pattern, which originally had an imitative value, was soon recognized as being visually pleasing for its own sake; and we can see Lorca attempting this style in his semi-cubistic drawings where the variation in pattern has a purely aesthetic value. Gris' synthetic cubism started with shapes and proceeded to experiment with them until the object emerged of its own accord; as he said:

> It is not a certain picture X which tries to enter into argument with an object, but an object X which tries to coincide with my picture.
>
> (Haftmann, 142)

Lorca is certainly trying to do this in some of his drawings (e.g. 40). It is an approach that can be compared to certain techniques in poetry, as for example when the poet does not mention an image precisely, but strings together a list of words so that gradually the image emerges. Writing of this kind occurs frequently in Lorca's *Poeta en Nueva York* (Poet in New York), for example in the second verse of *1910 (Intermedio)*:

> Those eyes of mine from nineteen-ten
> saw the white wall where the little girls peed,
> the bull's snout, the poisonous mushroom
> and an incromprehensible moon which lit up the corners,
> the pieces of dry lemon beneath the harsh blackness of the bottles.
>
> (OC 472)

This is not only a collage of verbal images, it also creates a visual image in a manner similar to a cubist painting.

During the course of his lecture on modern art (which was illustrated with slides) Lorca also praises Giorgio de Chirico. He finds that de Chirico's work contains a poetic element and that he explores new areas of feeling. There is a painting by de Chirico of a headless model wearing a tennis dress, a subject which also appears in Lorca's surrealist play *Así que pasen cinco años*. The aspect of de Chirico which probably interested Lorca most was his use of the *manichino*, the dehumanized symbol of the frozen world of things and the void around them. The thin dividing line between the animate and the inanimate, symbolized by the dress-dummy, was a favourite theme of artists at that time: the headless figure, the statue, the severed hand, anything human on the verge of becoming an object, is a subject explored by many surrealists, including Lorca, Dalí and Buñuel.

In the autumn of 1928 Lorca published the first and second sections of *Oda al Santísimo Sacramento* in the *Revista de Occidente*, which was run by José Ortega y Gasset. The whole approach of the poems is fairly unorthodox. The body of Christ contained in the host is described in vivid physical terms, 'like a child naked and panting'. In the second section, Lorca describes a horrific urban landscape, a world of solitude and lovelessness, to which only the body of Christ can give comfort. The poems were dedicated to Manuel de Falla who, being a devout Catholic, was shocked to be associated with such an experimental poem on a subject which to him was sacrosanct. He immediately wrote to Lorca expressing his surprise and total lack of identification with this particular attitude to Catholicism. The letter, though not harsh or unkind, was certainly distancing; and Federico and Falla were never again very close after this incident.

On 13 December 1928 Lorca gave a talk at the Residencia on *Las nanas infantiles* (see 2), in which he stressed the importance of working-class women in perpetuating the oral tradition of Spanish folk songs for children. But the days of the Resi were over for Lorca; all his old friends had dispersed. He would continue to stress publicly his friendship with Dalí, perhaps out of nostalgia or a kind of artistic insecurity, a need to convince himself and the world that he, like Dalí, was 'modern' and moving with the times.

Buñuel thought Lorca very traditional. He announced that he had a book of surreal poems in preparation, which would be called *Le chien andalou*, the name used among the inmates of the Resi for timid, traditional poets who dared not venture into the field of revolutionary poetry with a social content. The book was never published, but the title was transferred to the surrealist film that Buñuel and Dalí made together. Lorca felt that the title referred to him, although Buñuel later denied this; nevertheless there are scenes of male impotence in the film which probably refer to Lorca's homosexuality, and Buñuel said rather cruelly that the title was arrived at by himself and Dalí amid much mirth and laughter. This must have caused Lorca great distress.

In the autumn of 1928 one Cipriano Rivas Cherif had formed a theatrical company called the Teatro Caracol. They were a sort of fringe theatre who performed in a basement of the calle Mayor, the Sala Rex. They put on very *outré* shows, including Jean Cocteau's *Orpheus* and Rivas' own play about lesbianism, then considered a shocking subject. Rehearsals began for Lorca's *Amor de don Perlimplín con Belisa en su jardín* (The love of don Perlimplín for Belisa in his garden), a play about a middle-aged man who is persuaded to marry a girl half his age. On the morning after his wedding night, he is pictured wearing the traditional horns of the cuckold. Unfortunately, the theatre was closed down just as the play was about to open. The official reason given was the death of King Alfonso XIII's mother; but it is more than likely that the dictatorship of Primo de Rivera was applying a form of censorship. The authorities had not liked the theme of the previous play and they did not like the sound of Lorca's play either; in addition, the part of don Perlimplín was to have been played by a well-known retired army man turned actor, and this outraged the military establishment.

In April 1929 Lorca went to Granada for the opening of *Mariana Pineda* at the Teatro Cervantes in the square where the statue of his heroine stood. It was a great success; the applause was so enthusiastic that Lorca had to appear at the end of every act. The heroine, Mariana, was interpreted by the critics as being 'in love' rather than politically motivated, a commentary generally construed as a sop to the dictatorship of Primo de Rivera. At the close of the play, Lorca made a short speech saying that he felt *Mariana* was a work from his past. He alluded mysteriously to an 'impossible passion' that was destroying him; and he said he was trying to build himself up through his poetry, which nevertheless defended itself 'like a virgin'. Was this an indication that he was tortured by his homosexuality?

By now Lorca was enjoying more and more public success, but his private life was far from happy. His friend Aladrén was becoming involved with women. Federico grew so downcast that even his father became worried about him and, in an effort to cheer him up, offered to pay for him

43 *San Cristóbal* (St Christopher)

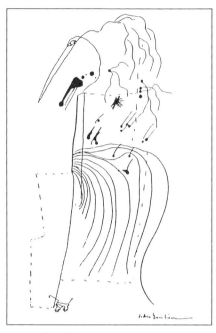

45 Bird and dog

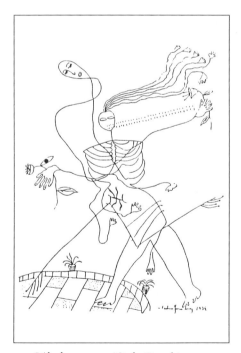

44 *Sólo la muerte* (Only Death)

46 *Esta es mi musa* (This is my muse) –
the classical profile at the top is part
of the Residencia letter-head

to travel. His friend Fernando de los Ríos was planning to go to New York, so Lorca decided to accompany him.

In May 1929 he was invited to open a public library in his native village, Fuente Vaqueros. All his family and friends were present, and there was great excitement and animation. Lorca spoke of the need for social co-operation, the need to sustain a spirit of well-being and happiness. He said he felt aware of the social injustice in society and that the only way forward was with the help of books. The whole event was a touching example of how Lorca was trying to overcome his own private chagrin through social involvement. His words demonstrate that he was not an ivory tower artist but that he felt the need to place his work in a social context, to justify the role of books in society both to himself and to others.

Lorca returned to Madrid for a few days before his departure for America. After a farewell dinner given by friends he left with Fernando de los Ríos and a niece of his who was going to school in England. They went to Paris and London, and made a brief visit to Oxford to see the historian Salvador de Madariaga. On 26 June 1929 they sailed from Southampton on the *Olympic*. During the voyage Lorca still had doubts as to whether he was doing the right thing, and wrote to his friends saying that he did not recognize himself, he seemed to be a different Federico.

FOUR

LITERARY DRAWINGS

When a subject is too long, or has a tricky poetic content, I resolve it with pencils.

F. G. Lorca

The *Olympic* arrived in New York at the end of June 1929. Lorca rented a room in John Jay Hall, a students' hall of residence at Columbia University. He had a vague plan that he might study English. Angel del Río, a professor at Columbia who looked after Lorca while he was in New York, recalled that he dressed in an aggressively 'tweedy' way, wearing shirts he had bought in Oxford and English sweaters with brightly coloured diamond patterns.

Lorca soon tired of the English language courses for which he had enrolled, and resigned himself to his inability to learn a foreign language. He mastered only a few words of English and those he pronounced badly. He preferred to get together with other Spanish-speaking people from the university and sing old popular Spanish songs which he had known since childhood.

In August 1929, during a visit to Vermont to stay with Philip Cummings whom he had met at the Residencia de Estudiantes, he worked intensely, but felt gloomy and downcast by the weather. Towards the end of August he went to stay with Angel del Río and his family in the Catskill mountains near Shandaken. He recounted that he had some difficulty in finding his way there. He arrived very late on the appointed day, leaning out of a taxi in which he had been driven around the hills for several hours. He had no money, so Angel del Río had to pay the accumulated fifteen dollars. Lorca added that the taxi driver had tried to mug him in a forest, a story which Angel del Río attributed to Federico's heightened imagination.

Lorca spent the rest of the summer with another professor, Federico de Onís, near Newburgh, before returning to Columbia in September. He now seemed quite contented with his life in New York and wrote back to Spain saying that he had regained his former high spirits and was working well. Together with his American friends he would visit the poor quarter of New York, Lower East Side and Harlem. His reaction to these places can be seen in *Oda al Rey de Harlem* and in the drawings done at this time (47, 48, 49, 50, 51).

The first impression we get from the New York drawings is the concern with death. But this is a strange and slow death, somehow almost unreal, which contrasts markedly with the type of death Lorca describes in *Romancero gitano*, and even more with the death of the bullfighter in *Llanto por Ignacio Sanchez Mejías*. In this poem death is seen as beautiful because the matador wills it upon himself: his way of life is a continual taunting of death. Lorca believed this to be the only way of dealing with life. He regarded the city dweller as leading only a half-life because he is not aware of the reality of death; therefore his life is unreal, a sort of micro-death in itself. In New York the distinction between life and death – and correspondingly that between reality and unreality – is blurred.

The contrast between the simplicity of Andalusia and life in New York is clear in the different imagery Lorca uses to describe the two places. In *Romancero gitano* there are only two opposing forces: freedom and the natural life, struggling against oppression and the unnatural life. Because the conflict is simple it is relatively easy to associate symbols with one force or the other: gypsies, honest causes and reality belong to the first, the civil guard, artificiality, patent leather to the second. But in New York the use of imagery is not quite so simple, precisely because of the blurred distinction not only between life and death but between reality and unreality. There is no cause which is entirely positive and consequently none which is entirely negative. We therefore find a considerable number of half-forces.

This confusion of imagery appears to echo the actual situation which Lorca finds in New York. Initially it seems that the main conflict is between the negro and the white man, almost repeating the theme in *Romancero gitano*. In fact, however, Lorca does not entirely favour the New York negro since he has lost his native heritage and is trying to become like the white man. Because of these conflicting attitudes, we are presented with a many-faceted view of New York which includes concepts of the negro in Africa, the negro in New York after the destruction of his culture, the white New Yorkers, and the First World War. These concepts arise by and large from the observation of external realities. From the poet's own interior world we have the concepts of freedom and the natural life, the poet as a child, and the poet as a young man.

A selection of drawings is discussed in more detail in the following pages because they are more closely related to particular poems and seem almost to work as illustrations to them. They represent visually ideas and associations which are later developed in the poetry in a more sophisticated form. The sequence of Lorca's creative process can be roughly described as, first, the idea or emotion, then the visual image or drawing, and lastly the verbal image or metaphor. The drawing is useful for understanding verbal images which might otherwise be difficult. It can stimulate the appropriate visual associations, and prevent the reader from making historical, etymological or other intellectual associations which would put him on the wrong track.

SELF-PORTRAIT OF THE POET IN NEW YORK (47)

This is the most comprehensive illustration of the New York dilemma, and its most striking aspect is the predominance of Lorca himself. He is represented both in the mask and in the creature flying between the buildings, and all the animals are directed towards or related to him. Lorca himself said in a talk, later included in the Barcelona edition of *Poeta en Nueva York* published by Editorial Lumen, 'I have said Poet in New York, and I should have said New York in a poet. I am that poet.' Lorca himself is the point of departure for all the attitudes which he depicts. His descriptions are a subjective reaction to the way in which New York affects him. (The New York poems were not finally published as a collection under the title *Poeta en Nueva York* until 1940, after Lorca's death.)

In both the New York poems and the drawings the mask has a dual role. It is associated with Lorca himself, and with the negroes, since he identifies himself with them to a certain extent.

The animals are also associated with the negroes in that they are an oppressed element and suffer in a similar way under the white man's rule. They represent nostalgia for Lorca's lost childhood and the absence in New York of the free and natural life. The animals are clearly small and

47 Self-portrait of the poet in New York

lost, like Lorca. They too are overshadowed by the buildings and, significantly, they are black. The symbolism of the animals is a source of much controversy. In the poems of *Poeta en Nueva York* it is not clear whether the animals are comforting or menacing. Often they are victims:

> The ducks and the pigeons,
> the pigs and the lambs
> place their drops of blood
> under the multiplications.
>
> (OC 516)

But often they threaten, perhaps as an act of revenge for their continued ill-treatment:

> The live iguanas will come and bite the men who do not sleep
> and he who flees with a broken heart will find on the corners
> an incredible crocodile lying still beneath the tender protest of the stars.
>
> (OC 493)

Similarly, the animals which Lorca draws seem both to comfort and taunt him. In drawings 53, 54 and 55 the horse-like animal is annoying the mask, and yet they seem to be inseparable.

The strange creature flapping about between the tall buildings is a symbol of Lorca himself, uprooted as he is in this very unnatural society. The creature resembles a sycamore seed in shape, an appropriate metaphor for the feeling Lorca wishes to express in this drawing: the winged fruit of the sycamore is carried by the wind as it falls from the tree, and after landing it breaks open to reveal a seed, which eventually takes root. The analogy with Lorca's situation is obvious: the poet is like a sycamore seed which is trying to find somewhere to land.

The plants in the lower left-hand corner seem to be withered and polluted. This is what happens to natural phenomena under the oppressive forces of an industrialized society.

The skyscrapers and their attributes are also important for their height and size and the fact that they are angular. They are sometimes interpreted as phallic symbols: the negress (symbolized by Night) has been dominated by the white man's technology:

A hive of windows machine-gunned the thigh of the Night

(OC 486)

The 'thigh of the Night' is a visual metaphor for the long narrow space of night sky between the tall buildings. Lorca compares this space of darkness to a thigh, with the rest of Night's body stretching out above the building. The personification of Night is repeated throughout *Poeta en Nueva York*.

On some of the skyscrapers in the drawing, the lines representing windows also describe numbers, and on one building they become letters of the alphabet. The numbers could be meant to signify quantity, the enormous amount of people, the sense of mass production, the vast scale on which things are done in America. They symbolize the impersonality of bureaucracy, expressed by the columns of figures in financial documents in Wall Street as well as by the tall buildings:

The mask will dance among columns of blood and numbers.

(OC 486)

The columns supporting the building on the right of the drawing provide an ingenious visual and symbolic contrast to Lorca's rendering of an urban park in the lower left-hand corner. The columns are aesthetically pleasing: highly decorated, verging on the gaudy, they are obviously man-made. They may also represent the metal supports that carry the city's elevated railway.

The black crescent moons represented in the central mask of the poet himself are simply poetic renderings of the many moles that Lorca had on his face. They associate Lorca with the moon's world, the cosmic forces.

The symbol of the mask relating to himself appears several times in the poems of *Poeta en Nueva York*; for example, in *Tu infancia en Menton* (Your Childhood in Menton):

Your distant solitude in hotels
and your pure mask of another sign.

and

> with the pain of an arrested Apollo
> with which I have broken the mask you wear.
>
> (OC 475)

Throughout the poem Lorca seems to be addressing love, or a state of mind suitable for love. The poem is recounted at various levels of mental awareness. Lorca is in an abyss of disillusion. He has just torn off the mask of love, in his frustration ('the pain of an arrested Apollo'), and has realized that love always wore a mask. But at least in his childhood he did not know it, so it was a 'pure mask of another sign'. The poem is an abstract account of love in terms of disillusion and deceit; Lorca was to recount this again and again in *Poeta en Nueva York* and in his plays. It describes a pure love, the love for another man, and refers to the spiritual relationship between men, as described later in *Oda a Walt Whitman*.

The other type of mask, which is associated with the negroes, reflects a similar problem in a wider context. Lorca speaks of 'Harlem in disguise', and then dedicates a whole poem, *Danza de la muerte* (Dance of Death) to this theme, with the refrain,

> The mask, look at the mask!
> How it comes from Africa to New York!
>
> (OC 484)

THE PARK (48)

This is a visual version of an idea in the poem *Paisaje de la multitud que orina* (Landscape of the urinating multitudes). The worm-like forms are Lorca's rendering of the multitudes – a derogatory portrayal, since these creatures are endowed only with urinating organs, male and female, which is all that Lorca considered noteworthy about them. Occasionally he has inserted a mouth which appears to be spitting or vomiting. It is a crude and bitter comment, as is the poem on the same subject. The poem does not actually repeat verbally the scene described in the drawing, but the drawing is certainly related to it, as in the line

> . . . These people who can piss around a groan
>
> (OC 490)

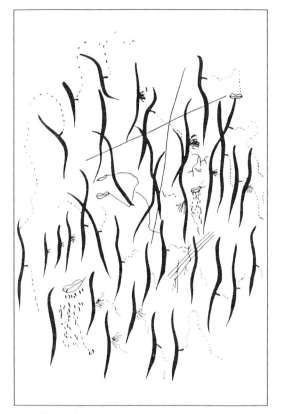

48 The park

49 Being with an empty stare

The drawing describes the point of departure or fundamental idea; in the poem the idea becomes much more complex. Lorca is describing the distance between the New Yorkers and all that is good, a lost paradise. I say 'distance' rather than 'conflict' because the two worlds never really come together, they are merely placed side by side for comparison. One of them is real while the other is only a dream. Lorca describes both in the same language, placing them in a mythical surreality. The ultimate mood of the poem, depressing though it is, is not pessimistic since the author denounces so positively the corruption of the city and celebrates the Garden of Eden as though it were retrievable.

BEING WITH AN EMPTY STARE (49)

> It will be necessary to travel through the eyes of idiots,
> open fields where tame cobras hiss,
> landscapes covered in tombs where fresh apples grow,
> so that the dazzling light may shine
> feared by the rich behind their magnifying glasses . . .
>
> (OC 490)

The verbal imagery in these lines from *Paisaje de la multitud que orina* relates to the visual images in this drawing. The 'idiots' of the poem are not fools but rather those who are traditionally uninvolved, innocent, pure; to a certain extent the poet himself, since he has insight into this world. The allusions that follow are almost biblical. The 'idiot' has a vision of the Garden of Eden after the Fall, full of serpents that are already 'tame' because sin and temptation are so prevalent in the society which Lorca is describing. This Garden of Eden is not a utopian paradise. It is adapted to suit, and possibly replace, the reality of New'York. There is death in this garden but it is more definite and real than in New York. The sinners succumb to temptation ('fresh apples') and this inevitably leads to death ('tombs'). But the cycle of life and death is clear in this garden.

Although there is no explicit reference anywhere in Lorca's work to suggest that the drawing illustrates the poem, they seem to have many images in common. The man's head would be the 'idiot', set against a desolate landscape of withered plants and box-like 'tombs' rooted to the ground. The plants emerging from these tombs enter the man's ears like telephone wires: in an industrialized society we are not only destroying the countryside but people's senses are being taken over by telephones and machines and these are ultimately connected with death.

WALT WHITMAN (50)

The question that arises from this drawing is Lorca's interest in Walt Whitman and in Anglo-Saxon literature as a whole. Lorca wrote a long *Oda a Walt Whitman*. As Professor Angel del Río says:

That he understood Whitman and had a clear idea of his message is evident in his Ode. The numerous repetitions, the chaotic enumerations, the length of the lines, the prophetic tone, the constant use of the first person, the great imaginative fluency and the cosmic breadth show without doubt that he had absorbed also a good deal of Whitman's style and mannerisms.

(Introduction to *Poeta en Nueva York* XXXI, Thames & Hudson 1955)

Lorca had understood Whitman's writing so well that he was upset to see him identified as a homosexual with the mindless, heartless homosexuals of New York. If Whitman is a homosexual, then to Lorca his is an idealistic Apollonian love:

> enemy of satyr
> enemy of vine
> and lover of bodies beneath the rough cloth.
>
> (OC 523)

In his ode to Whitman, Lorca wants not only to eulogize him but to show him as the antithesis of the squalor of certain areas of New York. The poem brings together two of Lorca's perceptions about America: New York and Walt Whitman. The two cannot be reconciled and yet they are linked not only by nationality but also by the theme of homosexuality. In his attempt to understand the problem Lorca realizes that it is not homosexuality he is denouncing but the 'fags of the cities'.

The style of this drawing is markedly different from all the other New York drawings. There is little distortion and no sign of ugliness or decay. Walt Whitman is shown as beautiful and serene, an idealistic figure.

The anti-urban theme is not a new one and can be traced back as far as William Blake, who foresaw the dehumanizing effect of industrialization in the eighteenth century: the paradox of man being imprisoned by a structure of his own invention. It has been pointed out that this conception of the United States had already penetrated into Hispanic verse long before Lorca wrote *Poeta en Nueva York*. The urban, industrialized aspect of the city cannot have been such a shock to him as is sometimes made out; he had undoubtedly read and heard much about New York before he went there. He and his friends were inserting references to

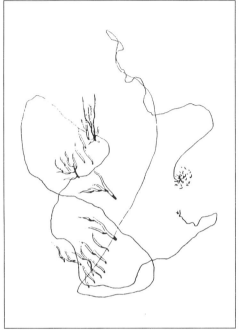

50 Walt Whitman

51 *El ocho* (Figure eight with trees)

America in their magazine *gallo* in 1928, presumably to shock the local provincialism of Granada by appearing modern. The fragmented 'surreal' style of *Poeta en Nueva York* was probably also self-consciously intended, since *Oda al Santísimo Sacramento* already contained traces of it.

While he was in New York, Lorca also added some finishing touches to *La zapatera prodigiosa* – a very traditional play based on essentially Spanish themes. He could not have been suffering a very profound nervous crisis if he was able to manipulate two disparate styles of writing simultaneously.

One of the people Lorca met in New York was Emilio Amero, a well-known Mexican graphic artist who was working as a commercial designer for Saks-Fifth Avenue and Wanamaker. Lorca used to attend cultural gatherings at Amero's 60th Street apartment with other Spanish-speaking friends. He would sing to them, play the guitar and recite poetry, and he particularly enjoyed these sessions because his poor command of English limited his contact with people.

At Amero's apartment Lorca was shown an experimental film made by Emilio called *777*. The film was an abstract study of shop machines. Lorca immediately responded to the medium and saw all sorts of possibilities for experimentation with imagery. He started inventing visual images to use in motion, and the resulting filmscript contains many of the same images that we find in the New York drawings and in the poetry.

The filmscript, *Un viaje a la luna* (see Appendix B), consists of a series of takes. The images it describes could have been used successfully in paintings, possibly by someone like de Chirico. As Angel del Río stated, 'more than in any other of Lorca's works the predominant form here is the substantive. These substantives are seldom abstract nouns but refer to all existing organic and inorganic beings and matter – animals, minerals, plants, natural phenomena, objects of the mechanical and man-created world – and also of the world of human desires and emotions.' (Introduction to *Poeta en Nueva York* XXVII). Perhaps the lack of movement in the filmscript can be explained by the fact that the movie camera in 1929 was still in its early stages of development from still photography. The predominance of substantives may be due to its visual, rather than conceptual, aspect. This is best observed by considering the images in the scenario. In the first take we have a 'white bed against a grey-walled background'. Over the bedcovers appears a dance of numbers, 13 and 22. This immediately recalls the poem *Suicidio en Alexandría* (Suicide in Alexandria) in which the same numbers are used as a sort of refrain. It is not their value that is significant; we are not concerned with their meaning, merely with the fact that they are numbers. Numbers are another kind of sign system, another symbol, and it is their incongruity in this context that interests Lorca. Like the razor slitting the eye in Buñuel's *Le chien Andalou*, unaccustomed groups of objects are intended to jolt us out of our established assumptions.

In the second take 'an invisible hand pulls off the covers'; but if it is invisible, how do we know it is a hand? There are many unresolved contradictions in these 'stage instructions', both technical and symbolic.

The images are mainly urban sexual images which present situations

Merienda.
Federico García Lorca.
1927

C16 *Merienda* (Snack)

52 Resuscitated man

53 Figure with black and white horse

of fear, eroticism, sexual initiation and corruption, with some references to Spain as well as to New York. The overriding theme is the lack of communication between people, and even between things, in the dehumanized society of New York. In take 54, men in dinner jackets are unable to pick up their glasses and the waiter pours wine until the glasses overflow; this suggests how things are failing to make contact. This view is echoed by the harlequin dancing with the almost nude girl, a paradox in itself since he is asexual. Also, in take 55, 'all the men are amazed' at the man with veins making 'desperate signs and movements which express life'. This is simply because the men do not understand life; the man with the veins is violent because this is the only way he can survive. Take 57 is lighthearted, a speedy recovery from take 56 and a reminder

54 Mask with black animal

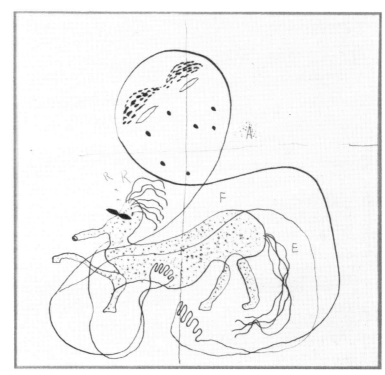

55 Mask with animal

that life goes on in spite of violence. There follows the tragic elopement of the harlequin and the girl, ending with his violent abuse of her. Observers and participants puke, symbolizing, one suspects, realism. The harlequin turns out to be the man with the veins who only dares to kiss the girl when she has become a plaster bust. This section shows how indebted to contemporary art many of the images are: plaster busts, harlequins, men in dinner jackets contrasted with nude girls: all this is very stylized.

The landscape of the moon is the final light relief after the very gloomy view of human relationships, full of hidden motives and double lives. Although the film is mainly about homosexuality, we discover in the end that the girl is in league with the man in the white dressing gown, who

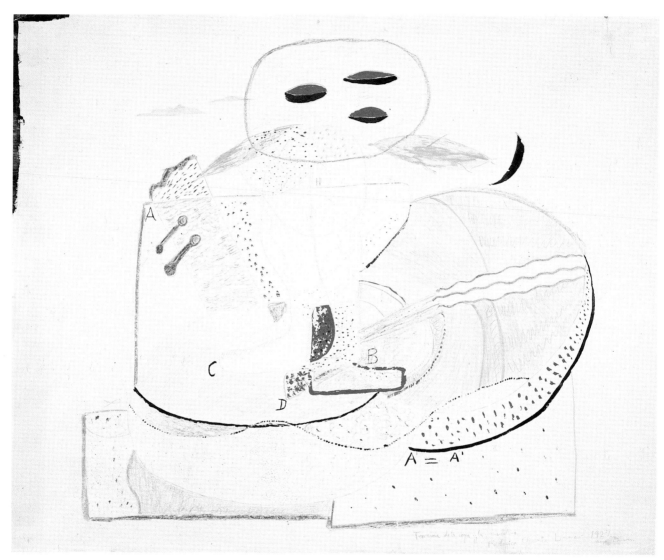

C17 *Teorema de la copa y la mandolina* (Theorem of the glass and the mandolin)

c18 *Naturaleza muerta* (Still life)

is the chief corruptor. We do not really know to what extent Lorca was identified with the view expressed in this filmscript. More likely than not he was consciously being stylistically experimental, as he was in the whole of *Poeta en Nueva York*, trying to live down his gypsy reputation.

In 1928 and early 1929 he had belonged to a cinema club in Madrid, organized by Buñuel from Paris, which showed, among others, the latest experimental French films. It is likely that these influenced Lorca in the writing of *Un viaje a la luna*.

In the spring of 1930 Lorca received a welcome invitation from the Hispano-Cuban Cultural Institute to lecture at various towns in Cuba. At last he could exchange the oppressive urban jungle of New York for a real one of luxuriant green plants and tropical flowers. Lorca felt at home in Cuba. He could speak his own language and enjoy the creole music and the beach parties. He spent much time in the home of a poetess called Dulce María Loynaz, whom he teased mercilessly about her serious attitude to art. He was feeling exuberant and full of vitality, and was in no mood to take life seriously. He had completely overcome the depression of the previous year.

The fact of getting away from Spain, getting away from Dalí, and leaving his broken love affair behind, strengthened Lorca's sense of identity. It is evident that there is more of himself in his New York drawings and poems; he is no longer hiding behind the personification of an insect or the image of the gypsy. There is much social observation in the New York poems, but Lorca is constantly trying to relate these observations to himself. On the personal level, he seems to have come to terms with his impulses. On the artistic level he has truly demonstrated that he can be as modern as any artist. Yet his success in universalizing his themes only reinforced his sense of nationality. By leaving Spain behind for a while, Lorca came to realize the extent to which he was a Spaniard.

FIVE

STAGE SETS AND COSTUMES

You already know what a lot of
pleasure it gives me to see myself
treated as a painter.

F. G. Lorca

On his return from America in June 1930, Lorca was full of life and eager to get down to work. His trip abroad had invigorated him and brought home to him the importance of being Spanish, not in the political sense but in the cultural sense. In the statements about his feelings for Spain Lorca never put forward nationalistic views. He emphasized moral values, saying that it was more important to be a good person than to be Spanish, and adding that he would always prefer a good Chinaman to a bad Spaniard. Lorca insisted that he belonged to the world and was brother to all.

In September 1930 he went down to Granada to see his family, but by December he was back in Madrid working on his American poems and supervising the production of *La zapatera prodigiosa*. It opened on 24 December in the Teatro Español, produced by the Compañía Caracol of Cipriano Rivas Cherif with Margarita Xirgu in the leading role. The play had only a short run because of growing political unrest: the monarchy was coming to an end and elections were about to take place. In 1931 the Second Republic was formed and Madrid was in a fever of political demonstration.

On 23 May 1931 Lorca published *Poema del cante jondo* which had been lying in a drawer since 1921. Hardly aware of the critical reaction, he then spent the summer in Granada, happily writing his first surrealist play *Así que pasen cinco años*. The title suggests that the action takes place over the course of five years. However, since all the events occur in the mind of the protagonist, Lorca is able to condense the action into the space of one evening, the implication being that a man can suffer as

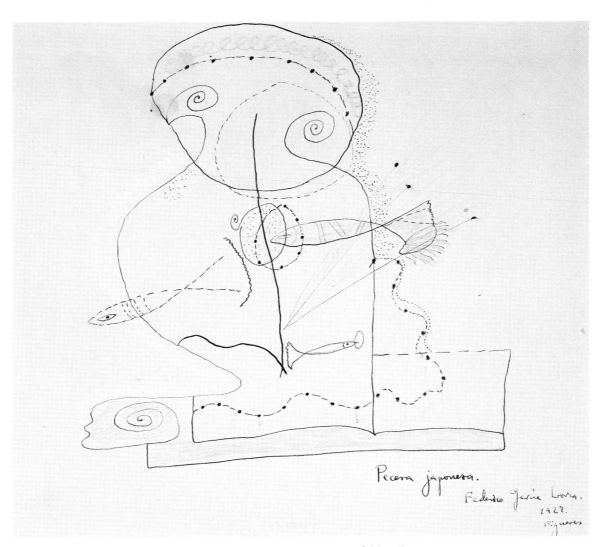

C19 *Pecera japonesa* (Japanese fishbowl)

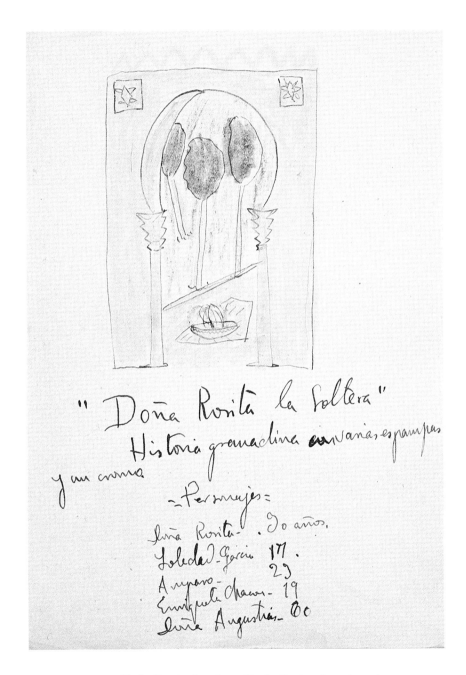

C20 *Doña Rosita la soltera* (Doña Rosita the spinster)

much in one evening as he can in five years. The main character, el Joven (the Young Man), consults different aspects of his personality by speaking to Amigo 1 and Amigo 2. He also imagines himself at different stages of his life, and appears as the Niño (Child) and the Viejo (Old Man).

The importance of the scenic effects and costumes in this play is considerable. The colours are carefully chosen. In the first scene, for example, el Joven wears blue pyjamas and is sitting in the library; the atmosphere is one of introversion and abstraction. This blue occurs many times in the play, always with connotations of spirituality. Towards the end of Act I the different characters are described in the stage directions by the colour of their fans:

> The Young Man has a blue fan; the Old Man a black fan; and the Friend an aggressive red fan. They fan themselves.
>
> (OC 1069)

This is a superb touch of visual drama. Each character is fanning himself with his own individual colour, or personality, and refusing to see the others' points of view.

From 1932 onwards Lorca dedicated himself almost entirely to the theatre, as director, musician and dramatist. His sense of social commitment on his return to Spain, coupled with his intense awareness of what it meant to be Spanish, moved him to form his own travelling theatre company called La Barraca. Its aim was to restore to the people of the Republic their own dramatic heritage. Lorca would tour the country with classics such as Cervantes' *Entremeses*, Calderón's *La vida es sueño*, Lope de Vega's *Fuenteovejuna*, Tirso de Molina's *El burlador de Sevilla* and many more.

The performers of La Barraca were university students. The group liked to emphasize the importance of democracy at the service of the people. The men wore blue overalls with a distinctive emblem designed by Benjamin Palencia in the form of a cartwheel on which was superimposed a black mask cut across by a white profile. The girls wore a blue dress with a white collar. Students could join La Barraca through an advertisement in the Central University of Madrid in the Calle San Bernardo. The preliminary audition consisted of a series of tests, devised by Lorca and his colleagues; applicants had to read a piece of prose or poetic drama, and recite a poem from memory. The actors were taken on and classified according to the roles they were best at: seducer, dangerous woman, gentle bride, unhappy man, traitor, monster, fiend, etc. The company was made up of thirty actors and technicians, eight of whom were girls. It was a unique theatre of its kind, not only because of the shows it offered, but because of the discipline, the enthusiasm, the cohesion, and the love of art that inspired all its members.

The project for the constitution of La Barraca was presented to the Union Federal de Estudiantes Hispanos in October 1931. At the head of the Ministerio de Instrucción Pública in those early years of the Republic was Fernando de los Ríos, ardent friend and admirer of Federico. He arranged for a grant of 300,000 pesetas to subsidize the maintenance and transport costs of the company. The troupe moved from place to place in a lorry. The sets were made by José Caballero, an engineering student, and Manuel Angeles Ortíz, an artist. The co-director was Eduardo Ugarte (whose chief characteristic was that he wore huge glasses), and he offered Lorca advice in all aspects of the running of the company.

Lorca's theatre drawings fall into two categories. First there are those to do with the mechanics of the theatre, the stage sets and costumes. Lorca participated mainly in designs for costumes (C22, C23, C25). Here his skill as a draughtsman was useful to him in a practical way. There are also many sketches for sets (56, 57, 59, 60). Such was Lorca's innate sense of theatricality that even when he was not designing a theatre set his drawings have a dramatic quality. His talent as a visual artist meant that he was able to conceive, create and express aspects of theatrical direction which normally have to be delegated to several other people.

The second category of theatre drawings is more concerned with the nature of theatricality and the function of the theatre as interpreter and purifier of experience. The mask motif expresses this theme. In his later plays Lorca questions the validity of each reality – the person, the mask, the mask's mask – and in being unable to accept any of these, begins to question the reality of the self.

Lorca's views on the role of the theatre and its connection with the theme of identity are expressed in his play *El público* (1933), which takes homosexual relationships as a point of departure for considering the questions of human love and the efforts of the artist to make contact with

C21 Mariana

C22 Theatre costume

56 Set for *Mariana Pineda* (part of a letter discussing the production)

57 Mariana on the scaffold

his audience. The play centres around the question of identity and the barely perceptible difference between theatre and life. In this respect it echoes the mask theme, for the actors are continually pulling off disguises (unmasking) to reveal different personalities underneath. There is much dialogue about accepting feelings of love, irrespective of the object of one's love, be it man, woman, or object. This notion of acceptance is transferred to the audience, who should, Lorca argues, accept the play on its own terms and not tear it to pieces through criticism. The play summarizes Lorca's feelings as a man and as an artist. It is the theatrical rendering of the mask motif which appears so frequently throughout his drawings.

Lorca's graphic work can be roughly divided chronologically into three periods. The early period before 1925 contains mainly very Spanish themes. This is followed by the Catalan period between 1925 and 1928 when he became interested in experimentation. The third phase, which

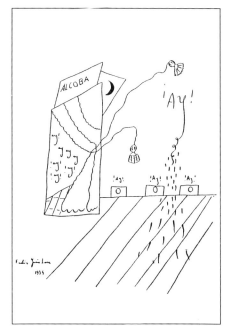 

58 Stage footlights   59 Set for *La zapatera prodigiosa*

includes the American experience, is altogether more personal and emotional in its statements. An exhibition at the Ateneo in Huelva, from 26
June to 3 July 1932, included eight of Lorca's drawings, and most of these,
with the exception of 'Spanish Dancer', 'St Christopher' and possibly
'Orpheus', seem to belong to this third phase:

La luna de les seminarists	The seminarists' moon
Asesinato en Nuevo York	Murder in New York
Bailarina española	Spanish dancer (c3)
Deseos de las ciudades muertas	Longings of the Dead Cities
San Cristóbal	Saint Christopher (43)
Orfeo	Orpheus
Muerte de Santa Rodegunda	Death of St Rodegunda (c27)
Parque	The Park (48)

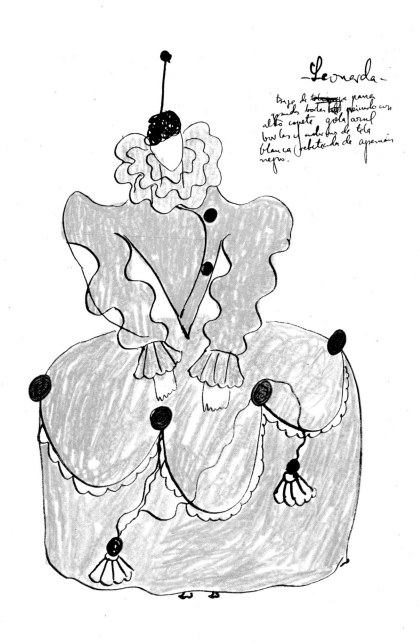

C23 Costume for Leonarda (from *La casa de Bernarda Alba*)

c24 Lemons

60 Set for *Mariana Pineda*

The exhibition also included drawings by Pablo Porras, José de la Puente, José Caballero and Carlos Fernández Valdemore. It was considered revolutionary, and also something of an insult, by the people of Huelva, a fairly small provincial town. They felt they were being teased and that the art on show might not be as serious as it pretended to be. But as José Caballero said, the aim of all those who had contributed to the exhibition was to educate the people of Huelva and to demonstrate the way of the new art. Their only mistake was that it was still too soon for Huelva.

In September 1933 Lorca went to Buenos Aires at the invitation of the Sociedad de Amigos del Arte to attend the successful staging of *Bodas de sangre*, performed by the company of Lola Membrives, and to give a series of lectures on *Juego y teoría del duende* (Game and Theory of the Elfin), *El canto primitivo andaluz* (Primitive Andalusian Song), *Poeta en Nueva York* and *Nanas infantiles*. Buenos Aires is a sophisticated city; Lorca attracted all the fashionable people, but soon learned to distinguish the serious people from the socialites. In frequent interviews he constantly recalled his native Granada, his childhood and his parents. The Argentinians, who are a formal people, were charmed by the simplicity of his manner and the fact that he was not carried away by his success; they were astounded by his natural behaviour, especially in allowing a reporter to interview him while he was taking a shower and then photograph him sitting on his bed. He returned to Spain in April 1934.

In October of that year the Republic was almost destroyed by a general strike, a regional revolt in Catalonia and a miners' strike in Asturias which, of the three, probably had the greatest emotional impact on the country because of the brutal way in which it was put down by the Moorish troops of Generals Franco and Goded. The uncensored right-wing press published horror stories of miners raping nuns and gouging out children's eyes. The left-wing press retaliated with tales of Moorish rape and accurate accounts of police and military brutality. Official figures estimated 1,300 killed and 3,000 wounded, but other figures claim 4,000 killed and 7,000 wounded. The country was polarized and frightened.

Lorca's success continued with the production of his play *Yerma*, the story of a barren wife whose husband may be impotent. Owing to the sensitive political situation it received a mixed press reception. Lorca had already made public statements about his attitude to his work and his feelings about the social order. On 15 December 1934 the national newspaper *El Sol* had published an interview with him in which he had expressed his solidarity with the workers.

'I know little, I know hardly anything at all.' I remember these lines of Pablo Neruda, but in this world I always am and always shall be on the side of the poor. I will always support those who have nothing, to whom even the peace of nothingness is denied. We men of intellectual background, raised in that middle class we call comfortable, are called on to make sacrifices. Let us accept them. The forces now pitted against each other are not human but telluric. I have in front of me, in a pair of scales, the result of this conflict. On the one hand, pain and sacrifice, on the other justice for all. In spite of the anxiety I feel about the future, which can be sensed but not known for certain, I come down on the side of justice with all the strength of my fist . . . What I hope for in the future is that the light should come from above, from the 'gods'. When those from above come down and sit in the orchestra seats, all will be in order'.

C25 Currito (from *Los títeres de Cachiporra*) – on the back
of another drawing taped to a mount

C26 A wood

After public statements such as these, it is hardly surprising that the critics' reaction to *Yerma* was based on the political bias of the newspapers they happened to represent, rather than on the play's artistic merit. The left-wing papers all praised it, whereas the right-wing press judged it unfavourably, claiming that it portrayed a woman in the grip of an obsession and that the unashamed celebration of sexuality in the play was distasteful. The play was discussed for months. It was thought by many to be immoral and blasphemous, and there was even talk of banning it.

In an interview published in a Madrid newspaper *La Voz* on 5 April 1936, Lorca's sense of social responsibility becomes very clear. The play to which he refers is probably an unfinished work known as 'Comedia sin título' (Play without a title), in which the pretence and fantasy of the theatre has been rejected. Art must have meaning and be relevant. These ideas are directly stated by a character called the Author, who harangues the audience, saying that he does not want to amuse them with words but rather to show them a slice of reality:

I am now working on a new play. It will not be like the previous ones. Now this is a work for which I cannot write anything, not a single line, because truth and falsehood have become unleashed and are floating around just like hunger and poetry. They have broken loose from my pages. The truth of the play is a religious and socio-economic problem. The world is brought to a halt by the hunger which ravages the towns. While there is economic imbalance the world cannot think. I have seen it. Two men walk by the side of a river. One is rich, the other poor. One has a full belly, the other pollutes the air with his yawning. The rich man says. 'Oh what a lovely boat on the water! Look, look at the lily blooming on the river bank.' And the poor man repeats, 'I'm hungry, I see nothing. I'm hungry, very hungry.' Naturally. The day that hunger disappears there is going to be the greatest spiritual explosion Humanity has ever known. People cannot imagine the joy that will burst forth on the day of the Great Revolution. Am I not speaking like a true socialist?

In June 1936 Lorca was conducting rehearsals for *Así que pasen cinco años* with Pura Ucelay, but because of the unsettled atmosphere in Madrid he decided not to put the play on. He felt the political climate was not right for the presentation of an experimental play with surrealist touches.

He told Pura Ucelay that only when three of his plays were playing simultaneously in Madrid would the public be on his side whatever he did, but at present they were not with him. In July he postponed the production until the autumn, giving vague reasons such as an intended trip to America, or possibly an unforeseen return to Granada. Sensing the mounting political tension, he attended gatherings to promote the defence of culture, and he publicly denounced nationalist ideologies.

Lorca remained undecided about whether to stay in Madrid or leave for Granada. One must bear in mind that he was now famous and that he had made his political feelings quite clear. His brother-in-law Fernández-Montesinos had been elected socialist mayor of Granada and this gave Lorca some confidence about returning. On the other hand, friends in power in the government advised him to stay in Madrid, saying that in times of crisis it is best to lie low, and that in a big city he was less likely to be noticed. He was advised to go anywhere rather than Granada, which had become polarized politically with a socialist mayor strongly opposed by Ramón Ruiz Alonso, a deputy of the CEDA (Confederación Española de Derechas Autónomas). The CEDA was a composite right-wing Catholic party, then the largest right-wing group, led by José María Gil Robles, a professor of law turned political journalist. The party view was very traditional and did not wholly approve of the Falange Español, another right-wing party founded by José Antonio Primo de Rivera (son of the dictator), a flamboyant character who described fascism as revolutionaly in its outlook: a new way of understanding the era. Many university students were attracted to the Falange. Ramón Ruiz Alonso, a typographer who early in his life had been frozen out of a job by left-wing unions, hated socialism with a passion. In April 1936 he had tried to join the increasingly popular Falange Español but although they would have been happy to receive him they were not prepared to grant him any special favours, so he remained in the CEDA. There were many falangists in Granada; some were friends of Lorca.

As the tension mounted in Madrid, Lorca decided to go back to Granada rather than do nothing. He maintained a fond childhood memory of his native town and could not quite believe that the conflict had penetrated even there. On 13 July, shortly before he left, he had lunch with his friend Rafael Martinez Nadal, who now lives in London, and

C27 *Muerte de Santa Rodegunda* (Death of St Rodegunda)

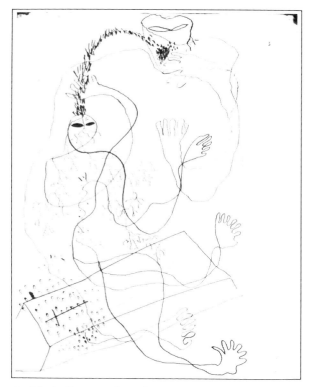

61 Mask, figure and tomb

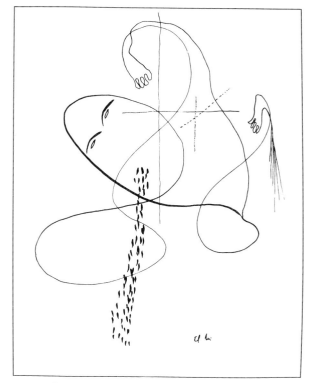

62 Mask

again communicated his indecisiveness about returning to Granada. He was afraid to stay alone in Madrid in the calle Alcalá; he would have to stay with friends if he remained. On the other hand he wanted to celebrate his Saint's Day with his father, especially since he knew that his father was without the company of any of his children.

On 17 July the garrison of Melilla rose up under General Franco who called on all nationalists to take up arms. Lorca was with his parents at the Huerta de San Vicente, their lovely country home just outside Granada. On 20 July the local government was taken over by the nationalists. The mayor, Dr Fernández-Montesinos, was arrested, accused of trafficking arms (although there were no arms to traffic). The only area of Granada to put up some resistance was the poor quarter of El Albaicín,

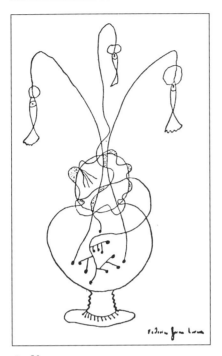

63 Vase   64 Vase

where the people fought back for three days. Many young people joined the falangists through fear rather than conviction.

Soon after the uprising, two men visited Lorca at his home. They claimed they were looking for a 'red' labourer but took the opportunity to intimidate Lorca, asking for his papers and ordering him to remain in the house to await further instructions from them. On whose authority they did this was not clear. Lorca was deeply hurt by this treatment from his fellow *granadinos*. Then, during a second intimidating visit, he was not only insulted but struck physically.

He telephoned his friend Luis Rosales, a falangist poet, to ask for advice. Again, as in Madrid, he was uncertain what to do. They talked of his leaving town, although as yet there were no clear political frontiers. No one imagined that it could be a matter of life and death. Lorca's elder sister Concha, the wife of Fernández-Montesinos, suggested that he should

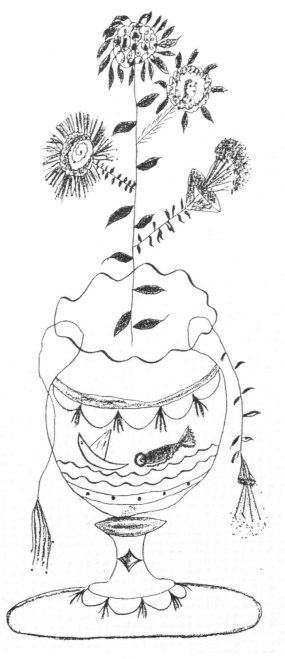

65 Vase

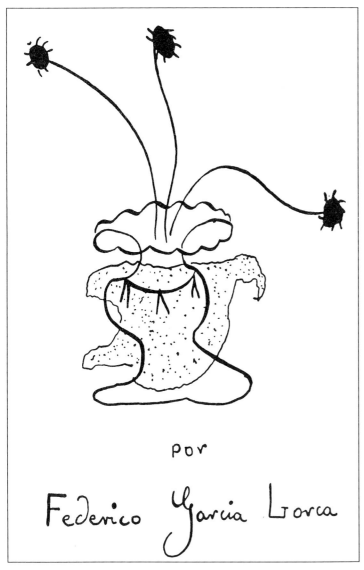

66 Front cover for *Romancero gitano* – the dotted area
represents the map of Spain

67 Signature

stay with the Rosales family. Who would think of looking for him in the house of a well-known falangist?

On 15 August the Rosales' home was surrounded by soldiers, Lorca was arrested by the CEDA and thrown into prison, accused of writing subversive works and being a friend of Russia. Many people tried to plead on his behalf, including Manuel de Falla. Lorca's housemaid took him food every day, until, on 20 August, she found he was no longer in his cell. He had been shot on the night of 19 August 1936.

There are many personal and political nuances in Lorca's death. Some say that there was an element of homosexual vengeance, but more likely it came about because of the rivalry between the CEDA and the falangists. By having Lorca arrested at the home of Luis Rosales, Ruiz Alonso was discrediting the falangists as well as Lorca.

The nationalists were understandably embarrassed by the gross mistake they made in shooting Lorca. For several days nothing was said publicly about the assassination by either political party. The killing was quite gratuitous, since Granada had fallen so easily to the nationalists. Eventually, on 30 August, Lorca's death was reported in a republican newspaper from Albacete. The news soon spread to Madrid where it was commented on with incredulity in *El Liberal* on 2 September. *El Sol* refused to accept the news and continued to hope that it was not true. The nationalists realized that their crime had horrified public opinion and tried to fudge the issue by pretending the socialists had shot Lorca. Similarly, the falangists made out that Lorca was on the point of joining their ranks and becoming a falangist poet. Rumours were spread that the civil guard had shot Lorca. All this cover-up activity points to the great esteem in which Lorca was held as a poet and artist, irrespective of his political views.

Lorca's concerns remained the same throughout his artistic career; he was trying to resolve the conflict between the confines and constraints of man's natural condition and his attempt to transcend and improve his lot. The tensions created by this clash recur again and again. Lorca's drawings, so close to the core of his personality, reflect his development as a person and as an artist. They are not political. They are a personal account of his drives and insecurities, a memento of his boundless energy and creativity, as well as a record of the sadness which lay behind the marvellously sociable entertainer.

There is a definite progression in the drawings, starting with the easy, naive style of his youth and adolescence, when the people represented often look sad or startled. We see the people of Andalusia, locked into their respective roles in society: dancers, traditional ladies, young men, nuns, mother and child. There is a sense of determinism about the way these people live out their lives. Later we see the struggle of the clown figure and the sailor, both associated with the mask theme, another aspect of Lorca's concern with the problem of identity in a judging society. Then comes a more experimental period with less human content, the result of his friendship with Dalí. It produced an altogether more stylized account of his experience, because Dalí encouraged him to depart from Spanish themes, even from reality.

To a certain extent the theatre drawings stand apart: they relate to the production of the plays in question, but they also tell us a great deal about Lorca's ideas and his attitude to his work. From the time of his visit to New York, Lorca returns to a more personal style, with a fairly morbid streak. We observe decomposing bodies, scenes of mutilation and vomiting. Lorca's horror of death was legendary among his friends. Dalí recounted how he used to enact the process of dying in an attempt to exorcise his fears (61, 62, C27). Perhaps the drawings are a presage of his own tragic end.

Would Lorca's drawings be of interest were he not a famous poet and dramatist? I believe they would, for they are undoubtedly sensitive and beautifully executed, with a marvellous understanding of line and colour. In Lorca's own words,

> You must look after the drawings well, so that when they are reproduced, the lines don't lose their feeling.

THOUGHTS ON MODERN ART

A LECTURE BY F. G. LORCA

'I paint as the birds sing,' said Claude Monet, the painter. This was the motto of the art world at the end of the nineteenth century. Painting was swamped in light and its surprises, drowning the beauty of form. Mass and the pure significance of outline had both been annihilated. The magic of light fell on all objects and destroyed them. This was the reign of impressionism. It should have been called sensationism or momentism, rather than impressionism. The beauty of the moment was exalted above all. The rushing river overcame the marble plinth. It was an era when paintings were looked at through a funnel made with the hand held up to the eye, when a face was nothing but a blob taking on the appearance of a face. Nature was imitated clumsily, using all the colours of the spectrum. Painters amused themselves with perspectives and other obfuscations, excluding any possibility of intelligent control, a drunken orgy of copying natural scenes. Painting was on its deathbed. But a reaction was stirring, and with that reaction came painting's salvation, a complete change of meaning for art. The last impressionists halted at their death leap and started copying the old masters and classical artists. They had to return to volume and to form, the fundamental requisites of painting. The backbone of painting had been lost: it had become a jelly which titillated the emotions and our childish sense of beauty. It was Cézanne who spoke these words, which became legendary, to a model: 'Sit still, sir, for I shall paint you just as I paint an apple.' From Cézanne sprang the constructivist spirit, which rebuilt painting until the scaffolding reached its pinnacle with Ozenfant and Jeanneret, and a style called purism. Another scientific extreme was achieved by the constructivists, who stated that 'one cannot determine the boundaries between mathematics and art, between a work of art and a technical invention'. Then a psychic reaction took place in painting: a spiritualist manner emerged, in which images were no longer provided by intelligence, but by the subconscious, by pure, direct inspiration.

In the past, painting had represented nature, that is, the 'conventional reality' of nature. Sight was a slave to what it saw, and the soul of a painter was a sad creature chained to his eyes, having no space or criteria of its own, unlike the souls of poets or musicians.

We needed a Perseus to kill the dragon and loosen the pitiful chains of this ancient Andromeda.

The first cubist painting was exhibited in a gallery in 1909. If I were to recount all the anecdotes, and the ridicule that was heaped upon it, I would need three days, and this is just a badly drawn-up simple sketch, because I haven't time for more. Let me just point out that the picture-framers did not want to frame it, nor did the barrow-boys want to carry it in their barrows. Who could have known that eight years later a painting of this kind would be sold for 300,000 francs?

With the advent of the first cubist painting, an abyss was created between the old painting and the new. For the first time, a large number of museum paintings were relegated to history, their proper category, taking with them all their supposed lively essences and eternal marvels. The battle between the old and the new had begun. Picasso was still painting in a realist style which, although admirable and work of the deepest Spanish understanding, was picturesque, and, thank God, soon to be superseded. [Slide projection of the old lady and the Aragonese girl.] Braque had a wonderful talent, as most people and artists in other media all agreed. Meanwhile, the cubists wanted to jest and to drive a few unfortunate sober citizens crazy; and thank God for their humour! The cubists were achieving the greatest, most purifying, most liberating work yet to be realized in the history of painting. They were salvaging painting. It had been an art of representation and they were converting it into an art in itself. A pure art, released from reality. In the painting of the past, colour and volume had been at the service of portraits and religious paintings. In modern art, colour and volume began to be valued for themselves for the first time ever. They communicated with each other and inter-related on the canvas, obeying their own laws.

The poets Guillaume Apollinaire and Max Jacob started a similar movement in poetry. In painting, the genial Pablo Picasso from Málaga, and some other painters, were the first really to advance through undiscovered territory. This was painting which cried out, which affirmed, which moved the world because it was seen by everyone and appeared all over Europe. It was disconcerting and inspiring, like everything that is alive and contains hot blood.

1919. The Great War destroyed reality as we knew it. What we saw was incredible. Reason could not withstand the war. Reality did not seem authentic. Ethical constructs came toppling down. We no longer believed in our old values. All the old fetters were loosened and the soul without asylum was alone, naked, responsible for its own perspective. We should not believe our eyes, they deceived us. We should free ourselves of natural reality and look for its true pictorial counterpart. We should not search for the real representation of an object, but find its pictorial expression, its geometric or lyrical expression, and the appropriate quality of its material. The Great War gave birth to modern art. Through pain, reality was overwhelmed by an abstract force, and painting ceased to be a slave to the senses. It became something autonomous. Painting had been the same for five centuries. Now there was a definite swing in a more logical direction, one which was more in keeping with the meaning of creation.

Another Spaniard, Juan Gris, spoke these very logical words at a famous lecture at the Sorbonne: 'It is very easy to paint a glass bottle exactly as it is, and render its texture faithfully. The glass blower, as he makes his bottle, does it much better than I can. But I am looking for the pictorial expression of glass, and the pictorial texture of glass, not its visual reality.' In fact, objects possess certain attributes and innuendoes which are not at all pictorial. The painter must eliminate these since they are useless and damaging. For example, reflections, those revolting little touches of white which old-fashioned painters gave to objects. This is the greatest visual nonsense, since sheen is a fleeting tremor outside the object, forming no part of its outline or volume, and therefore alien to its nature. Of course old-fashioned painters are looking for the viewer who might say, 'So and so has painted Joe Bloggs and has caught him exactly. If I came across the painting in a room I would get such a fright, etc.', things which have nothing to do with painting.

We escape from the destructiveness of the impressionists and we arrive at the Franciscan school of the cubists. We come upon greens, reds and yellows in all their variety, leaving behind the mauves and the veiled nebulosities which saturated the pinks and greys, the infinite silvery colours of the impressionists. Now we see dark grey, white, siena, tobacco, and other muted, austere colours from the cubist palette. The orgy of colour has come to an end. What used to be the most important thing no longer exists, the old criteria for painting no longer matter. They used to say, 'this picture represents this'. That was fundamental to historic painting. Now we are in another hemisphere. Now we say, 'this is a painting which does not represent anything more than a painting', just as in poetry a sonnet does not represent anything more than a sonnet, and a chair does not represent anything more than a chair. But what does the painting mean? What does it express? That is another matter. A grey provides a background against which various shapes and solids play and intermingle in a beautiful harmony felt by the painter, and their separate identities create a world which moves and stimulates thought in the viewer.

We have departed from reality to arrive at this type of creation. Just as the poet creates his own verbal image, so the painter creates his own visual image, which fixes and generates its own emotion. The artist only needs a few objects to work from. He detaches himself from them and recreates them. He improves on them, he discovers their secrets, their pictorial centre, which the copy artist cannot perceive.

The cubists were austere in their creations. They composed most of their still lifes with nothing more than a violin, an apple, a plaster hand, or an old sea salt's pipe.

But they rendered these objects in a thousand ways, using the most wonderful, tactile, grainy materials, which make you feel like eating the work or running your hand over it. Georges Braque combines oil paint with sumptuously fine sand, not dissimilar in texture to a fine English sports cloth. Our own Juan Gris expresses himself in a cold, spare, schematic way, reminiscent of the perfect emotion of a moonbeam, or guitars strung together by the delicate sentiment of nocturnal fish. This is pure matter, pure form, and pure colour. How distant from the pictorial concept of the old-fashioned portrait painter!

Now painting is free. It has been raised to the spiritual rank of an art form which is self-sufficient and independent of all external influences, utilizing its own resources to the full.

Picasso and Georges Braque are the leaders of the wartime generation, the originators of the cubist family tree, whose last branch is now in the sky, pure and definite, in the shape of Juan Gris, from whom all the constructive and truly pictorial elements of today are growing.

Besides cubism, which is, I repeat, more than mere painting (an unusual, absolutely new creation within the confines of the visual arts), various other schools are emerging which, using the language of colour, are creating (careful!) not visual art as some people are pretending at this blessed moment, but literature, and very often bad literature. One of these is Italian futurism. Futurism exalts movement, it wants to make its paintings vibrate on the vortex of a great dynamic force. Futurism hates the statue, and loves the runaway horse. It brings together external sensations and is no more than a celebration of motion. Nothing could be more genuinely Italian. There is no great difference between a futurist and a speaker at a public meeting. Marinetti, its founder, is just that: a wonderful orator who dared to speak ill-sounding words on a solemn occasion. Its painters, Balla, Corsi and Soffici, had more talent than Marinetti, but futurism cannot really justify its existence, because now we have the cinema. Film has given us a visual moving spectacle, something which the futurists could not render on their canvases. A Twentieth Century Fox newsreel, such as we see in the cinema every week, surpasses all the creations of those admirable Italians who did so much to awaken their country. They wanted to burn the museums and break Michelangelo's statue of David in order to save Italy from the horror of tourism. Italy writhes beneath this curse, vanquished and stared at by people who have no more feeling for art than to say, 'this painting is worth four million', and 'that pulpit would cost £400,000'.

Dadaism sprang up in the mid-war period. This was also literary painting to my way of seeing things. Works were created for the moment. They came face to face with all art forms, and had a joyous reaction. They neither affirmed nor negated. It was a necessary purge, and those who did it continue to be people of wonderful talent. But one must admit that dadaism was a six-day wonder, in spite of the great commotion that it created; it was of great significance as a destructive agent. Futurism and dadaism have been battlefields, elements of scandal, bound up with political ideas and urban movements. But while the dadaists dispersed to return to their old disciplines, or to try new ones, Marinetti gave futurism an official sanction when another great futurist, Mussolini, embraced him beneath a sixty-metre flag donated by the people of Milan.

After the war, there were painters such as the purists and constructivists who followed the cubist discipline, taking painting to scientific extremes. Others formed a movement of social painting which castigated vices, presenting them in all their horror. These were the German realists, those unbearable German realists. Others converted painting into an expressive celebration of reality, the ultimate spirit of things: the expressionists lit up the Berlin of their time, as they still do. There were too many 'isms'. Some were literary, quite beautiful, and of recognizable artistic value, others were pure visual images which adhered to the cubist discipline. It was a studious discipline without excessive public controversy. Works of thoughtful maturity were produced for exhibition.

The really regenerative movement was cubism in its three phases: discipline, love and law. Death to perspective and an abstract exaltation of volume. This was its profile. By 1926 cubism had been accepted. The cubist lesson had been completely absorbed. But then a sad cerebralism, a tired intellectuality invaded painting. Severini and Gris knew their paintings back to front before they executed them. Where could we go? Towards instinct, chance, pure inspiration, the fragrance of the direct.

The surrealists began to emerge and to abandon themselves to the ultimate heartbeats of the soul. Now painting is freed from the disciplined abstractions of cubism and, master of the accumulated technique of centuries, enters an uncontrolled mystical period of supreme beauty. People begin to express the inexpressible. The sea fits into an orange, and a tiny insect can astonish the entire harmony of the planets where a recumbent horse bears a disturbing footprint in his fine eyes beyond mortality.

After the rigid objectivity of the 1920s, painting now arrives, very old and very wise, at a lyrical plain where she must necessarily follow a biological process and shed her ancient skin, to emerge naked as a child art, sister to cave paintings and first cousin to the exquisite art of primitive tribes.

The glory of having produced the three greatest revolutionary artists of contemporary painting falls to us Spaniards. The father of all existing painters is the Andalusian Pablo Picasso, the man who has created the theology and academy of cubism. Then we have Juan Gris from Madrid, and the divine painter-poet Joan Miró, child of Catalonia. The racial characteristics in all of them are quite apparent. Picasso is the genial Andalusian with miraculous powers of invention and remarkable intuition. Juan Gris is Castilian, all reason and burning faith. He was converted to cubism and has practised nothing else until his death, which sadly occurred last year. While Picasso was painting in a cubist style he was simultaneously making pictures in the manner of Goya, or executing a Fragonard, or a Mantegna, with prodigious technical ability. Juan Gris was a grey man who studied his painting without touching on a single point of dogma. Joan Miró is more European and his art is now quite unclassifiable because he has too many astronomical elements to adhere to any particular nationality. But there is no doubt that Spain continues to pour forth her genius in torrents. Her genius for eternal life, which lights up and will always brighten man's activities with her own particular and unusual glow.

In this brief summary I have not the time to expand the subject as I should like to. It is vast, and this is no more than a sketch of modern art. Many ideas suggest themselves but I must confine my thoughts. Nor do I want to bore the audience with quotations and names of new artists from all over the world. No-one has surpassed the three figures of whom I have just spoken. I am going to project some more slides now. Not too many, so as not to tire people.

Impressionism	1	Renoir
	2	Cezanne
Cubism	3	Picasso
	4	Picasso
	5	Gleizes
	6	Juan Gris
	7	Leger (decorative)
	8	Ozenfant (aseptic, already a scientific theory)
	9	Proun (change from painting to architecture)
Futurism	10	Severini 1913
	11	Balla

Optical Cubism   12   Kandinsky

Dada   13   Picabia

In Giorgio de Chirico we begin to notice the poetic influence in painting. He is a strange painter. He owes a lot to the cubists and he creates an art which he calls metaphysical, which attempts to resolve the following problem: to render the immaterial by means of matter. He succeeds, to my way of seeing things. I think Chirico produces a new emotion of disquiet, solitude and terror in his paintings. Jean Cocteau, that delightful French poet, has said, 'Chirico or the scene of the crime, Chirico or the moment of danger'. Yes, his canvases convey just this anxiety. They are canvases with a simultaneously strange and deadly feeling:

14   Chirico

15   Chirico

Now let us pass on to a few examples of surrealism. Here we have the young Dalí, lightly influenced by Chirico:

16   Dalí

17   Miró

18   Miró

In these last two paintings by Miró, we are in the presence of the purest art form that has ever been attempted since men picked up their brushes. It is not a passion. This statement of mine can be demonstrated both within a historical context and on a purely aesthetic level. This nocturnal landscape where insects speak to one another, and that other panorama, whatever it is (because I don't mind not knowing, I don't have to), are on the boundaries of reality. They come from a dream, from the centre of the soul, where love is made flesh and incredible breezes of distant sounds can be heard. When looking at these paintings of Miró's I experience the same mysterious and terrible emotion that I feel at the bullfight at the moment when they plunge the spear into the crown of the beautiful animal. This is the moment when we hover on the borders of death, when death pierces the tender and intangible tremor of grey matter with her steely beak.

There is no doubt that modern painting is a tangible reality which includes all the countries of the world. As always when we are talking about a great movement, people from all over the world can concur without actually agreeing. The proof of this overwhelming force is that the attitude of the old-fashioned painters, exemplified in their exhibitions, is no longer of any interest to anybody. These frightened and sordid old painters who don't wish to look properly and don't want to know about their failure, cut themselves off to copy our marvellous, inimitable reality, which then destroys their canvases. Old-fashioned painting is consuming itself in a dramatic retreat. There are cases such as that of a great painter from Granada who had the best taste and subject-matter in my opinion, but when he found himself in the midst of the earth-shattering movement of modern art, he abandoned his painting, not wishing to embrace any new artistic disciplines (and in this he did wrong); he merely waited, with great nobility, hoping for a change in his sensibility. This attitude describes one of the rarer spirits, and it also reveals the total failure of nineteenth-century art and, with it, that of all historical painting. All the styles of painting have now been mastered, with total success and technical ability. Modern art is setting out in a new direction, which we must encourage.

Art will never disintegrate, and I feel real pity for those artists who do not fight and discipline themselves. They dream impossible dreams which they want to come true. That is why I feel terribly sorry for those old painters who spend all day copying and recopying their models, to earn their daily bread without any effort, or joy, or pain. I would burn their pictures and throw the artists out into the street to struggle with the burning energy of man and the passionate love of God.

Art has to advance just as science does, day after day, into that incredible field which does become real, towards the absurd which does become a pinnacle of truth.

Before drawing to a close, I should like to say that my position is an honourable one, that I have faith in what I say, and that neither the sniggers of ignorant people, nor the smears of madmen, nor anything else, worry me at all. Not one bit. Faith and joy in a beautiful future are firmly anchored in my conscience. Ladies and gentlemen: my sketch of modern painting has ended.

Granada 1928

FILMSCRIPT: A TRIP TO THE MOON

BY FEDERICO GARCÍA LORCA

Scenes:

1   A white bed against a grey walled background. Over the bedcovers appears a dance of numbers, 13 and 22.

2   An invisible hand pulls off the covers.

3   Big feet run rapidly, wearing exaggerated long stockings of white and black.

4   A frightened head looks toward a point and fades into a head made of wire with a background of water.

5   Letters saying HELP! HELP! and moving downward, with a double exposure of a woman's sexual parts.

6   A long, narrow passage with a window at the far end, surveyed by the camera.

7   View of an avenue (Broadway) by night, with flashing signs,

8   Which all fades into the preceding scene.

9   Two legs oscillate rapidly

10   The legs fade into a group of trembling hands

11   The trembling hands fade into a double exposure of a little boy who is crying

12   And the little boy fades into a double exposure of a woman who is giving him a beating.

13   This scene fades again into the long narrow passage through which the camera runs rapidly backward.

14   At the end, a large design of an eye upon a double exposure of a fish, which fades into the following:

15   Through a window passes the rapid fall of a double exposure of letters in blue, HELP! HELP!

16   Each HELP! HELP! sign fades into a foot print

17   And each foot print into silkworms upon a leaf on a white background.

18   From the silkworm emerges a large skull and from the skull a sky with a moon.

19   The moon divides and there appears a sketch of a head which vomits and opens and closes its eyes and which dissolves into:

20   Two little boys who are walking along singing with their eyes closed.

21   The heads of the little boys are covered with ink spots.

22   A white expanse on which are sprinkled drops of ink.

23   A door.

24   A man in a white dressing gown comes out. From the opposite side comes a boy in a bathing suit dotted with large black and white spots.

25   A large shot of the suit, upon the double exposure of a fish.

26   The man in the dressing gown offers a harlequin suit to the boy but he refuses it; then the man catches him by the neck. The boy screams, but the man stops up his mouth with the harlequin suit.

27   Everything fades out on a double exposure of snakes, this into crabs and this into other fish, all rhythmically.

28   A close-up of a live fish held in the hand of a person who squeezes it until it dies, and then advances toward the camera with its little mouth held open until it covers the lens.

29   Within the fish's mouth appears a large design on which two fish leap and palpitate in agony.

30   These are converted into a kaleidoscope in which a hundred fish leap and palpitate in agony.

Legend: TRIP TO THE MOON

31   A room in which two weeping women dressed in black are seated wtih their hands lifted to heaven and their heads thrown upon a table where there is a lamp.

32   A sketch of their breasts and hands, their long hair is thrown over their faces and their hands are deformed with spirals of wire.

33   The women continue to raise and lower their arms.

34   A frog falls upon the table.

35   A double exposure of the frog seen on a background of orchids which are waved furiously; the orchids are seen and a woman's outlined head which vomits, rapidly nodding positively and negatively, negatively and positively.

36   A door is slammed, and then another and another and another upon a double exposure of the weeping women who are lowering their arms.

37 As the doors close, upon each one can be read a sign which says: Elena, Helena, Elhena, elHeNa.

38 The women go rapidly toward the door.

39 The camera, with an accelerated pace, descends the stairs and, with a double exposure, ascends them.

40 A triple exposure of the ascent and descent of the stairs.

41 A double exposure of iron bars that pass over a sketch which represents the 'Death of Roelejunda'.

42 A woman in mourning falls downstairs.

43 Large shot of her.

44 Another very realistic view of her wearing a handkerchief on her head in the Spanish manner.

45 Her head face down with a double exposure upon a design of veins and grains of salt, this one in relief.

46 The camera from below focuses upon and goes up the stairs. At the top appears a nude boy whose head is like an anatomy card. The muscles, veins and tendons are all seen sketched upon the nude figure.

47 He is dragging the harlequin suit

48 And appears with half his body showing, looking from side to side.

49 The preceding fades into a nocturnal street scene in which three overcoated figures are making signs of feeling cold. Their coat collars are turned up. One looks upward at the moon, lifting its head; the moon appears upon the screen. Another figure looks at the moon and the head of a bird appears in full flight. He twists its neck until it dies in front of the lens. The third looks at the moon; on the screen a moon appears, outlined on a white background which fades into a male sex organ and then into a screaming mouth.

50 The three figures flee through the street.

51 In the street the man with the veins appears, lying with his arms outstretched.

52 The preceding fades into a criss-cross of a triple double exposure of fast trains,

53 The trains fade into a double exposure of piano keys and hands playing,

54 These fade into a bar occupied by several fellows dressed in dinner jackets. The waiter sets glasses of wine before them but the glasses are so heavy they are unable to raise them to their lips. An almost nude girl enters, and a harlequin: they dance. The others try to drink again but cannot. The waiter pours the wine until the glasses overflow.

55   The man with the veins appears, gesturing and making desperate signs and movements which express life; all the men are amazed.

56   A head looks stupidly about, approaches the screen and fades into a frog; the man with the veins squeezes the frog between his fingers.

57   A sponge appears and a bandaged head.

58   The preceding fades into a street in which the girl, dressed in white, is fleeing with the harlequin.

59   A head which vomits appears

60   And immediately all the people in the bar vomit.

61   The preceding fades into an elevator where a little negro boy is also vomiting.

62   The harlequin boy and the nude woman ascend in the elevator.

63   They embrace.

64   A view of a sensual kiss.

65   The boy bites the girl on the neck and violently pulls her hair.

66   A guitar appears and a hand quickly cuts its strings with a pair of scissors.

67   The girl defends herself from the boy who with great fury gives her another profound kiss and places his thumbs over her eyes as if to plunge them into their sockets.

68   The girl screams and the boy, with his back turned, takes off his jacket and a wig and the man with the veins appears.

69   Then she fades into a plaster bust and the man with the veins kisses her passionately.

70   The plaster bust is seen with lip prints and hand prints upon it.

71   Again the words Elena, Helena, Elhena, ElHeNa appear.

72   These words fade into screams which appear on the screen in a violent fashion.

73   And these screams dissolve upon the man with the veins, dead upon discarded newspapers and herrings.

74   A bed appears, and hands which cover a corpse.

75   A fellow in a white dressing gown and rubber gloves, and a girl dressed in black comes in. They paint a moustache on the dead man's head and kiss each other amid great bursts of laughter.

76   A cemetery bursts from them and they are seen kissing over a tomb.

77   View of a cinematic kiss with a background of other persons.

78   And finally . . . landscape of a moon with trees swaying in the wind.

CHRONOLOGY

1898	Born 5 June at Fuente Vaqueros, near Granada.
1898–1908	Childhood in Fuente Vaqueros, Asquerosa and Almería; birth of brothers and sisters, Luis (who died very young), Francisco, Concepción and Isabel.
1909–15	Secondary education in Granada at a private school and the local grammar school. First studies in music: guitar, piano and harmony.
1915	Graduates from grammar school. Begins to study law and literature at the University of Granada.
1916	Two archaeological expeditions with Martín Domínguez Berrueta through Andalusia, Castile and northern Spain.
1917	Death of Antonio Segura, FGL's music teacher. Interruption of music studies, and family opposition to his studying in Paris.
1918	Publication of *Impresiones y paisajes*
1919	Moves to Residencia de Estudiantes in Madrid.
1920–23	Exams in Granada for law degree, obtained 1923.
1920	Production of *El maleficio de la mariposa* in Madrid. Manuel de Falla moves to Granada; friendship with FGL.
1921	Publication of *Libro de poemas*.
1922	*Cante jondo* festival and competition in Granada.
1923	Marionette session to celebrate Festival of the Magi in Granada.
1924	Project to produce *Cristobica* and *Mariana Pineda*. Meets Pablo Neruda.
1925	Stays with Dalí in Cadaques and Figueras; reads *Mariana Pineda* to Dalí family.
1926	Lecture on *La imagen poética de Don Luis de Góngora* at the Ateneo in Granada.
1927	Works on production of the magazine *gallo* in Granada. First night of *Mariana Pineda* in Barcelona with sets by Dalí. Exhibition of drawings at the Galerías Dalmau in Barcelona. First night of *Mariana Pineda* in Madrid.

1928   Project to publish drawings and poems together with Dalí, edited by Sebastián Gasch.
Publication of *Romancero gitano*.
Lecture on *Imaginación, inspiración, evasión* at the Ateneo in Granada.
Lecture on modern art, *Sketch de la pintura moderna*, at the Ateneo in Granada.
Lecture on *Las nanas infantiles* at the Residencia des Estudiantes in Madrid.

1929   Prepares sets for *Don Perlimplín*.
First night of *Mariana Pineda* in Granada.
Leaves for America via Paris, London and Oxford.
Resident at Columbia University; writing *Oda al rey de Harlem*, *Ruina*, *Nocturno del hueco*, and fragments of *La zapatera prodigiosa*.

1930   Invited to lecture in Cuba. Writes *Son de los negros en Cuba*.
Returns to Spain. Production of *La zapatera prodigiosa* in Madrid.

1931   Publishes *Ruina*, *Niña ahogada en el pozo* and *Ciudad sin sueño*, later part of *Poeta en Nueva York*.
Plans to form travelling theatre company, La Barraca.

1932   Performances by La Barraca in Burgo de Osma, San Juan del Duero, Madrid, Galicia, Asturias, Santander, Granada, Alicante.
Exhibition of drawings at the Ateneo in Huelva.
Reads *Bodas de sangre* to Carlos Morla Lynch.
Lecture on *Poeta en Nueva York* in Barcelona.

1933   First night of *Bodas de sangre* in Madrid; repeat of *La zapatera prodigiosa*; first night of *Amor de Don Perlimplín con Belisa en su jardín* in Madrid.
Invitation to Buenos Aires to lecture and attend productions of *Bodas de sangre* and *La zapatera prodigiosa*.

1934   Visit to Montevideo. Writing *Yerma*.
Returns to Spain via Rio de Janeiro. La Barraca performs in Jaca, Madrid and Santander.
First night of *Yerma* in Madrid.

1935   Production of *Bodas de sangre* in New York.
Reads *Llanto por Ignacio Sanchez Mejías* at Teatro Español, Madrid.
Finishes *Doña Rosita la soltera*.
First night of *Yerma* in Valencia.

1936   Rehearsals for *Así que pasen cinco años* (never performed in FGL's lifetime).
Finishes *La casa de Bernarda Alba*.
Leaves Madrid for Granada.
Execution of FGL's brother-in-law, Manuel Fernández-Montesinos.
Execution of FGL 19 August by order of Ramón Ruiz Alonso.

SELECT BIBLIOGRAPHY

LORCA, F. G. *Obras completas*, Madrid 1966

LORCA, F. G. *Poeta en Nueva York*, trans. Ben Bellitt, London 1955

LORCA, F. G. *Cartas a sus amigos* (Introd. Sebastián Gasch), Barcelona 1950

LORCA, F. G. *Cartas, postales, poemas y dibujos* (Introd. Antonio Gallego-Morell) Madrid 1969

GENERAL BACKGROUND

BRETON, A. *Manifeste du Surréalisme*, Paris 1947

BRETON, A. *Le Surréalisme et la Peinture*, New York 1945

CIRICI-PELLICER, A. *Miró y la imaginación*, Barcelona 1949

DALÍ, S. *The Secret Life of Salvador Dalí*, London 1948

DUPIN, J. *Joan Miró*, London 1962

HAFTMANN, W. *Painting in the Twentieth Century*, London 1965

HAGSTRUM, J. *The Sister Arts*, Chicago 1958

HATZFELD, H. *Literature through Art*, New York 1952

KAHNWEILER, D. H. *Juan Gris, his Life and Work*, London 1947

KYROU, A. *Luis Buñuel*, Paris 1962

MARINETTI, F. T. *Le Futurisme*, Paris 1911

MUNRO, T. *The Arts and their Interrelations*, New York 1949

READ, H. *Parallels in Painting and Poetry*, London 1936

READ, H. *Surrealism*, London 1936

CRITICAL WORKS

AUCLAIR, M. *Enfance et mort de Federico García Lorca*, Paris 1968

CANO, J. L. *García Lorca*, Barcelona 1962

CORREA, G. *La poesía mítica de Federico García Lorca*, Oregon 1957

DURÁN, M. *Twentieth Century Views on Lorca*, New Jersey 1962

GEBSER, J. *Lorca, oder das Reich der Mutter*, Stuttgart 1948

GEBSER, J. *Lorca, poète-déssinateur*, Paris 1949

GIBSON, IAN *El Asesinato de García Lorca*, Barcelona 1979

GIBSON, IAN *Federico García Lorca*, Barcelona 1985

LAFFRANQUE, M. *Les Idées Esthétiques de Federico García Lorca*, Paris 1968

MASINI, F. *Federico García Lorca e la Barraca*, Rocca San Casciano 1966

NADAL, R. *El Público*, Oxford 1970

PRIETO, G. *García Lorca as a Painter*, London ?1949

PRIETO, G. *Dibujos de García Lorca*, Madrid 1949/55

DEL RÍO, A. *Poeta en Nueva York*, Madrid 1958, Cuadernos Taurus No. 8

RODRIGO, A. *García Lorca en Cataluña*, Barcelona 1975

INDEX

INDEX